GOD'S WORD IN A CHILD'S WORLD

GOD'S WORD IN A CHILD'S WORLD

*Messages and Guidelines for
Sharing the Gospel with Children*

ELDON WEISHEIT

AUGSBURG Publishing House • Minneapolis

GOD'S WORD IN A CHILD'S WORLD
Messages and Guidelines for Sharing the Gospel with Children

Copyright © 1986 Augsburg Publishing House

Scripture quotations unless otherwise noted are from the Good News Bible, Today's English Version, copyright 1966, 1971, and 1976 by American Bible Society. Used by permission.

Library of Congress Cataloging-in-Publication Data

Weisheit, Eldon.
  GOD'S WORD IN A CHILD'S WORLD.

  1. Children's sermons. 2. Preaching to children.
I. Title.
BV4315.W3727   1986   252'.53   86-2442
ISBN 0-8066-2214-8

Manufactured in the U.S.A.   APH 10-2745

   2   3   4   5   6   7   8   9   0   1   2   3   4   5   6   7   8   9

CONTENTS

PREFACE

One need not do a deep study of Luke 15 (the parables of the lost sheep, the lost coin, and the lost son) to know the joy of finding something that has been lost. We've all done it.

Those parables also remind us of the joy we feel when a friend finds something that has been lost. When they tell us the good news about finding the lost, we celebrate with them.

I have discovered a third joy, not mentioned in Luke 15, regarding finding that which has been lost. It is a joy to find something and give it to the person to whom it belongs. That's why I enjoy preaching children's sermons.

Each time I study a section of Scripture, I find something. That's why this "how to" book on children's messages insists that every message must start with a study of God's Word. You need to find something.

Think of the treasures you can find in the Scripture: God's grace, victory over sin and death, the power of the Holy Spirit, God's love, wisdom, guidance, and comfort. You can find your relationship with God and with people. You can find your own self-worth and values. You can find your roots in history and your promise for eternity.

The joy of finding these things is that they are for you—but not only for you. First, you can rejoice about what you have found for yourself. Then, you can celebrate your find with others. Then, the third joy, you can give what you have found to others, because it belongs to them.

The key to understanding the need and purpose of children's messages is that the Word of God belongs to them. It is not our generosity that moves us to do the work and provide the time for children's messages. What we have found in God's Word belongs to the children.

If you are reading this book, you are obviously interested in preaching the gospel to children. I encourage you to do it with the joy of one who has found something that must be shared.

This book is the result of 15 years of writing children's messages. During that time I also have had the opportunity to do many workshops about preaching to children in many parts of the country and in various denominations. I thank all who have participated in those workshops. Your stories, questions, and encouragement have added to this book. These workshops have also given me a positive view of the holy Christian church. Seeing people of great diversity share a common interest in teaching the message of Christ to children also helped me see that the church still has a unity—and a future.

While publishing this book ends years of writing a children's message every week, it will not end my preaching of children's messages. I thank both the children and the adults who are glad to remember their childness at Fountain of Life Lutheran Church, Tucson, Arizona, for the help and encouragement they have given me in my ministry to them and through my writing.

Chapter 1

WHY CHILDREN'S MESSAGES?

Why use children's messages? For some, children's messages have already become a tradition. We used them last year so we'll use them this year. To others, children's messages are the latest fad. If nothing else has worked to build up sagging church attendance, we'll try children's messages.

Anyone using, or considering using, children's messages should have better reasons than habit or desperation. Worship services are the most unifying part of any Christian congregation. The worship services need to be planned so that they achieve the purpose of bringing all the people closer to God and closer to one another.

Children's messages are not an instant cure for all the problems that can develop in a congregation's worship life. However, if those who plan the worship for a congregation spend some time thinking about why they have—or don't have—children's messages, they may discover some things that will help other areas of worship also.

Children Are a Part of the Church

The most obvious reason for children's messages is that children are a part of the church. Children in a worship service are not like uninvited offspring who gatecrash a wedding reception. They are not brought along to church only because the parents couldn't find or afford a baby-sitter.

The church is the body of Christ. It is people for whom Christ gave his life on the cross and for whom he rose from the dead to give eternal life. The door of the church must be open to the same people to whom the heart of Christ is open. Through the church God brings people back together again.

The worship service is where the unity is created and expressed. When members of a Christian congregation gather for worship, they are the body of Christ assembled. The people experience togetherness with one another. Their unity is a witness to others and an invitation for others to become a part of the body of Christ. Their witness to the world is shown by whom they welcome—and also by whom they exclude. If they exclude anyone whom Christ has invited, they are dividing the body of Christ.

Using children's messages is one way to help children feel they are a part of the body of believers—and also a way for adults to recognize children as their brothers and sisters in Christ. Of course, the same logic could be used for specialized sermons for other groups in the congregation. Can you imagine the pastor of a congregation saying, "I invite all the widows to come up front for a special sermon for them"? Or, "Will all the engaged couples come up for a sermon"? The list is unlimited, but time and patience are not. Forget the idea of a sermon for each identifiable group in the congregation. However, each group that might feel excluded should be made to feel welcome, not only by the words of a sermon, but by the actions of a congregation.

But maybe the needs of children are special. Adults can easily see that their needs were considered in the planning of the worship service. The seats were made for adults. The Bibles, hymnals, bulletins are all planned for the adult world. Adults are in charge of the music. They lead the worship. They even pass the offering plates—often right past the eager eyes and hands of children. One can understand why children might get the idea that they really aren't welcome at a worship service.

A children's message says to every child, "We knew you were coming and we have planned for you." Even the children who are too young to understand the intellectual point of a children's message still know they were included. They need to feel that they are a welcome part of God's family. Being in Sunday school and other educational programs is important for children, but it is the worship service that will provide the continuity into their adult lives. People whose childhood experience bonded them only to the educational programs of the church often leave the church—and return only when they have children old enough for the educational programs. If, as children, people are bonded to the worship activities of the congregation, they are connected with an experience that will continue all their lives.

In the Old Testament the children were regarded as a part of the chosen people. They were a part of the congregation. Each Jewish boy was circumcised when he was eight days old. No one asked him if he wanted to be Jewish. The parents were not forcing something on their child. Being Jewish was a gift from God. It would have been wrong for them to withhold such a blessing. It was a sign of God's covenant with them.

The Jews took the meaning of circumcision seriously. Children were a part of the worship life of the people. Through the prophet Joel God told them:

> "Blow the trumpet on Mount Zion;
> give orders for a fast and call an assembly!
> Gather the people together;
> prepare them for a sacred meeting;
> bring the old people;
> gather the children
> and the babies too.
> Even the newly married couples
> must leave their home and come" (Joel 2:15-16).

When the people gathered for an assembly they listened to long readings from Scripture. The small children could not understand what was being read. The babies would cry and distract others. But they were invited because they belonged to God's family. Their earliest memories would include being held by a parent in the assembly of God's people. It was a part of their lives as much as other childhood experiences.

Children are part of God's family. They belong to the church. The children's message is one way to let children know they are welcome in worship services. It gives the children a sense of participation. It builds memories that bond them to a worship experience that can be repeated throughout their lives.

Adults Listen Too

Those who use children's messages in the regular worship services of a congregation soon find a second reason for including a short, extra sermon for children. The adults listen too. When church members quote a sermon in classes, meetings, or counseling sessions, it is most often the children's sermon. When they talk about a sermon to friends and family members who do not attend church, it is most likely that they will speak about the children's sermon.

Several things about children's messages make them more digestible and memorable to the adults in the congregation. In my own experience of preaching children's messages for over 24 years and writing 15 books of children's messages, I have learned to apply principles for writing children's sermons to my other sermons as well. Having learned to preach to children, I think I now do a better job of preaching to adults.

First, a children's message, by definition, is short. Instead of preaching the entire message of a text, the pastor selects one idea and applies it to the lives of the hearers. When asked how many points a sermon should have, one preacher responded, "At least one." For a children's sermon the answer would be, "No more than one."

A short, clear message is easier to understand and to remember than a long, involved sermon. Too often the main point of a regular sermon is lost in the attempts to give all the interesting relationships of the readings of the day, the depth of understanding that the preacher has gained from knowing the Greek or Hebrew language of the original text, and the clever things that learned theologians have had to say about the text. In children's sermons there is no time for all of that. The message is, "God said." The application is, "This is what it means for us."

Children show us when they have lost interest in something. Their eyes and hands move on to other things. Adults, though they have learned in school to appear to be listening when they are not, do not have long attention spans either. Their minds also wander to the week that is past and to the one that is coming. A short, direct message is more likely to hold their attention and get filed in their memory banks.

Second, the language used in a children's message is more easily understood than that in a sermon prepared for adults. To children sin is "doing something wrong," not "antisocial behavior." Love is "God likes to be with you," not "a manifestation of the incarnation."

Speakers and writers who really understand what they are talking or writing about can explain what needs to be explained in the language of their hearers. If an idea cannot be put into the vocabulary and thought pattern of the hearers, there is no point in trying to communicate the concept.

Those who preach often speak in the language and thought patterns of the books they read and the training they have received, rather than the language and thought patterns of their hearers. This is not saying that the hearers are all uneducated. Many may be more educated than the one doing the preaching—but most often not in the fields of theology, personal relationships, and spiritual growth. They need to be impressed, not by the education and wisdom of the speaker, but by the message of God's love for us in Jesus Christ.

The most influential and memorable statements in history and in literature are short and to the point. The preacher has a better chance of making such statements in a children's message than in a general sermon.

Third, the children's message often uses an object lesson, story, or other device to serve the hearer as a string around the finger to aid the memory process. Everyone knows it is easier to remember what one sees than what one hears. Any audio message that is connected to a video message will be remembered better than the verbal message alone. When people can see a sermon as well as hear it, they are increasing their participation in the message by using both the sense of sight and the sense of sound. The sense of touch (Example 26), taste (Example 5), and smell can also be used to increase the understanding of the message by the hearer/watcher/toucher/taster/smeller.

The Old Testament prophets Jeremiah and Ezekiel made frequent use of object lessons. Read Jeremiah 13 to see how he used linen shorts and a wine jar to help the people see his message. Also read about the broken jar in Chapter 19 and the basket of figs in Chapter 24. Ezekiel used his object lessons in parables. Read the parable of the vine in Chapter 15, the eagles and the vine in Chapter 17, and the corroded cooking pot in Chapter 24. The objects used by these prophets first help us understand their truths; then they help us remember what was said.

Jesus also used objects to help his hearers/viewers understand and remember the truths he wished to teach. Think of objects that have special meaning because Jesus used them in his teaching: fish, seeds, vines, sheep, salt. These words have special places in Christian art and literature because our Lord used them as object lessons.

Most adults appreciate the object lesson as well as children—but not all. I wanted to write my seminary thesis on the use of object lessons in the Sunday morning service. The idea was rejected (and therefore remained unwritten until now), because, in my professor's opinion, object lessons were regarded as a method of education for primary students and would be insulting to adults. My experience has proved otherwise. Twice I have served congregations with a number of university professors sitting in the pews. They were the ones who most often appreciated the children's message.

Some people will still object to the use of children's messages or visuals in any sermon. Their objections should not be ignored. Some have changed their minds after they have seen a few. Others need to consider the issues raised in this chapter about the worship life of the entire congregation. And some will never appreciate children's messages. Some people do not think visually or conceptually, they understand only a linear method of communication. Their limitations should not be imposed on the entire congregation; however, such people should not be regarded as unspiritual or negative. People who are tone deaf are not that way on purpose, but they should not dictate the music program of the congregation. In the same way those who have limitations in understanding varieties of communication should not limit the methods of communication.

In my present congregation, where we have multiple services, the solution is to include the children's message in the major services, but not in the minor ones. In other congregations children's messages could be used at noncommunion services or according to some other agreed schedule. The important point is that an effort to share the love of Christ should not become a divisive issue in a congregation.

All Christians can grow in an understanding of worship when they come to realize that the worship service cannot be planned for each individual. Corporate worship gives us an opportunity to show our concern for others. If something is included in a worship service that one person does not like, that person faces a special opportunity: he or she can give that part of the service to others by being aware that it helps them. By the way, this applies to hymns, Bible translations, forms of liturgy, and many other things in worship that may appeal to some but not to others.

To Children, for Children, and through Children

Another reason for using children's messages as a part of the regular diet in a congregation's worship program is this: the messages are not only *to* children—they are also *for* children.

The messages speak *to* children in order to give them a truth of law and gospel from Scripture. One of the functions of the church is to speak a message to its people. The church has a message to speak to children.

But the messages are also *for* children in that they speak for the children to others who are present. Radio and TV evangelists and guest preachers can speak *to* people, but a parish pastor also speaks *for* his or her people. Each person comes to church to receive truth and to give truth. When children are in church, the pastor must also speak for them so that others who are there will benefit from their presence (Example 1). The awareness of this purpose of children's messages came from a study of Matt. 18:1-5:

> At that time the disciples came to Jesus, asking, "Who is the greatest in the Kingdom of heaven?"
> So Jesus called a child, had him stand in front of them, and said, "I assure you that unless you change and become like children, you will never enter the Kingdom of heaven. The greatest in the Kingdom of heaven is the one who humbles himself and becomes like this child. And whoever welcomes in my name one such child as this, welcomes me."

We have long understood the responsibility of adults to provide for children. In addition to the physical needs that all parents provide for their children, Christian parents have the responsibility of teaching their children the way of life and eternal life through Jesus Christ. The reading from Matthew's gospel says that children also have something to give to us. All adults need to become like children; they need their childness.

We receive our childness from children, just as they receive their adultness from us. The children in a worship service are there as a part of the body of Christ. They receive from others in that body; they also give to others in that body. Many adults seem to instinctively know they need childness. I know senior citizens who have driven away from retirement villages in order to worship in a congregation with children present. I know single adults, both male and female, who appreciate the attention given to children in worship even though they have no personal investment in the children.

Children have not been adults. They cannot read the adult's books; they cannot jump into the adult world. However, all adults have been children. They can read the child's books. The adult can get down on the floor and play with a child's toy, but the child cannot drive the adult's car.

To understand the process of human development, consider the rings of a tree. By looking at a cross section of a tree, one can see the size and shape of the tree at any age of its life. Each year the tree adds a new ring, while it also retains all its previous ones. Inside every 90-year-old tree, one can see 89 other appearances of the same tree.

In the same way, each person adds another year to life on each birthday. When the six-year-old becomes a seven-year-old, the six-year-old is not gone. All the experiences are still there. Another year is added. So it happens with each birthday. The adult who forgets his childhood has a hollow core in his life. The 50-year-old adult needs to reach back through all the previous years to have a complete life. All adults need their childness.

The children's message helps the adults see and hear the child in themselves. The subjects are from a child's world and spoken to the child's need. And the truth of Christ reaches back through each adult to the child in that adult. The adult remembers who he or she was and then has a better understanding of who he or she is.

The U.S. Department of Defense, through its military chaplains, produced a film showing 10 outstanding preachers, each preaching in his own congregation. The film has 10 excellent sermons. The viewer sees not only the preacher, but also the congregation. Many of the congregations had no children present; none of them had many children in the worship service. There was no distracting noise that children make. All the people appeared to be camera-ready, without the wiggles that children add. But what would those 10 pastors have done with Matt. 18:1-5?

Any sermon, children's or otherwise, preached in a congregation belongs to the people who hear it. It is *to* them; it is *for* them. It is also to be preached *through* them. The sermon must be delivered in a language and a thought pattern that the people can use as they take the message to their family and friends. Most parish pastors are concerned about church attendance. Their concern is relieved if they preach *through* people as well as *to* people, because the people attending receive a sermon in words and thought patterns that they can use to pass the message on to others.

Some who teach and preach to children tell jokes about children who misunderstand what they are taught. You may have heard the one about the holy family's plane flight to Egypt with Pontius as the pilot. Or the one about the child who knows God's name is Howard because he was taught to pray, "Howard be thy name." There is a sadness, however, about such jokes. Most of them are based on the church language we so often use to communicate the faith. Christ came to speak to the world, and those who follow him are sent to the world with his message. When we leave other buildings, we "go out," but from the church we "go forth." We "stay" with our friends, but we "abide" with Jesus. Any pastor who talks about Jesus riding "on an ass" is seen as naive at best, and stupid at worst, by 10-year-olds.

The pastor who wants to preach through people must speak in words and in thought patterns that people can take home and explain to others. A simple test: many people who are in church will have family members who did not come with them. If those who stayed at home asked those who attended what the sermon was about, could each hearer repeat the message of the sermon? The sermon should be delivered with that "second generation" of hearers in mind.

A children's message offers one of the easiest ways for a pastor to preach through people as well as to people. That is when the sermon is theirs—not just because they hear it, but also because they can share it.

More Than Messages for Children

What has been said about children's messages in this section applies to more than giving a five-minute talk to a group of children in the chancel. It speaks to an attitude about worship. The inclusion of a concern for children does not mean an exclusion of anyone else. It is not children versus adults. It is not the sermon against other parts of worship. Worship belongs to the people of God. For God to be praised, God's Word must be spoken to the people, and they must respond with praise. Everyone who preaches must find the best way to get the Word to the people in a way that they see the power of God in their lives. Then those who hear will praise the Lord.

Chapter 2

PREPARING THE MESSAGE

A message for children does not start with an object looking for a truth; it is a truth looking for a way to be proclaimed, understood, and used.

The Text

The first step in preparing a sermon for children is to select the text. If the message is to be from God to God's people, it comes from God's Word. The power of the message comes from the Scripture used. The Word of God is the source of the creativity and the excitement of the message.

The preacher who depends on his or her own knowledge and energy as the source of sermon material will soon run out of resources. The sermons will repeat the same limited number of themes, and the messages will lack the "new song" excitement that is always a part of proclaiming the gospel. Therefore, every sermon starts as a message from God to the preacher. As the preacher studies the text, he or she receives again the faith that comes from "hearing the message" (Rom. 10:17).

After the message has been applied to the preacher's own life, the preacher is filled with the creativity and power of the text. He or she then has a resource to give to others.

A prayer I like to use as I start work on any text to be used in a sermon or class is: "Holy Spirit, as you have inspired the writing of this Word, so also inspire my study and use of the Word. Amen."

One of the easiest ways to select a text is to use a lectionary of assigned readings from the Psalms, Old Testament, Epistles, and Gospels for each Sunday of the church year. Following such a system gives both the preacher and the congregation a well-planned, balanced diet of God's Word. An assigned series of texts helps the preacher avoid falling into a rut and repeating a few limited themes that he or she thinks are especially appropriate for children. Some assigned texts will be about subjects difficult for children. That difficulty is an important part of the challenge of preaching to children. For example, some lessons are about divorce. Though that is a difficult subject for a message for children, it is a necessary subject in the lives of young people today. Such texts give the children a chance to hear about divorce in church and to have the gospel of Christ connected to the subject.

Usually the entire reading of a lectionary selection cannot be used as a text for a children's message. A single verse or sentence makes a better text, especially from an Epistle or other reading that does not tell a story. Select the part of the entire reading that has a spiritual truth for children. Even if ideas from the rest of the reading are used, it is often better to keep the text short for the sake of children. It is more difficult to select a short section from a Gospel lesson or other reading that has a story. Again look for a single statement or idea that introduces or summarizes the story. You may need to tell other parts of the story but read only a short section as the text.

Using a lectionary of assigned texts is also helpful when the children's message is a part of the regular Sunday worship of a congregation. If the main sermon is on one of the assigned lessons and the children's sermon is on one of the other lessons, there will be a relationship between the two sermons. Each sermon can be used to reinforce and relate to the other. Examples or objects used in the children's sermon can be referred to in the other sermon. The use of a children's sermon does not have to take up more time in the service; it becomes a part of the main sermon—which can then be shorter.

All children's messages need not be based on the assigned readings for the day. Children's messages give a good opportunity to bring nonchurch holidays (Examples 32-34) and other current events (Examples 36 and 40) into the service.

Another source of texts for children's messages can be found in other sections of Scripture referred to in the main sermon. Often a preacher will use other Bible passages to help the hearers understand the point of the text. A children's message on one of those other parts of the Bible will help the congregation understand the relationship of the two sections of Scripture (Example 17). The context of the text for the main sermon also makes a good text for a children's sermon. The verses immediately before or after an assigned text often help explain the lesson. Using one or more of those verses as the text for the children's sermon will add to the main sermon. (Example 3).

Children's messages may also be used as a part of special emphasis in congregational programs, such as evangelism (Example 11), education (Example 12), stewardship (Example 13), and social ministry (Examples 14 and 15).

The Translation

Next, the best translation of the text must be chosen. If the pastor and/or congregation uses only one translation, the decision is easy. However, the children's message may offer an opportunity to make all who worship aware of the fact that more than one translation of the Bible exists (without making an issue of the fact).

Some people believe it would be better if a congregation (or the entire church for that matter) used only one translation of the Bible. The consistency would make it easier for those who quote Bible verses and for people to remember where stories and verses are in the Bible. It would also avoid the discussions about differences in translations.

However, people should be aware that a variety of good translations is available. Comparing several translations is a good method of Bible study. People who have used only one translation often find it difficult to adjust when another is used. When only one translation is used over a period of many years, people often identify the authority of God's Word with the translation—as in the attitude of many about the German Bible (in my own tradition) and the King James Version.

While the Bible itself does not speak of translations, it does give us a good example about the attitude toward them. Those who wrote the New Testament and those who are quoted in it had a choice of two translations of the Old Testament. They could use the Hebrew/Aramaic of the original Scriptures, or they could use the Septuagint, a Greek translation of the original language. They did not use only one or the other, but frequently quoted from each without reference to their source. More importantly, no one ever argued about which translation was being used. They discussed the message of the Word— not the language in which it was written. Perhaps the use of several translations in a worship service would help the hearers understand the use of translations, and focus the attention on the meaning of the message.

In choosing a translation for the children's message, several things should be considered:

● Use a translation, not a paraphrase, of the Bible. Children's Bibles and other paraphrases can be helpful to the person preparing a children's message. They give examples of language at the proper level for children. They give ideas for applications. They are a good resource for studying the text, but use a standard Bible translation for the text.

● Use a translation that has words most easily understood by children. A translation that is best for one text might not be the best for another. Watch for words that would be difficult for children to understand. Part of any sermon is to define the meaning of a word as it is used in the text. Choose a translation that uses words that children already know and understand. Watch for words that may have a different meaning when used in the text than when used by the children in other parts of their lives. For example, *fear* to children means "being scared." While *reverence* is a longer word and may need an explanation, it is not misleading.

● Use a translation that gives the children words they can repeat in their daily lives. If the message is given to them not only for their own spiritual growth, but also for their Christian ministry to others, it must be in a language they can repeat. Words and phrases from the text give the hearers a way to pass the message on to others. I once heard a Sunday-school teacher complain about a modern translation "because when the kids read that, they understand it themselves, and there's nothing left for me to teach." I think that is a marvelous testimony for the modern translation. The children should hear the Word in a way that they can speak the Word.

The Children

The formula for a sermon is: the Word + the People = the Sermon. A sermon that is based only on the Word of God may be theologically correct and intellectually strong, but such a sermon may be totally unrelated to the people who hear it. A sermon that articulates the feelings of people will reach their minds and hearts because it deals with their joys and problems. But such a sermon only helps the people see things as they are. For a sermon to accomplish its purpose, the Word of God must be applied to the lives of people. Those who hear the sermon must see things as they *are* and also as they *can be* with the help of Jesus Christ. The message of the Scripture must move through history until it reaches what is happening at that moment in the lives of the worshipers.

Therefore, each children's message must be prepared for the children who hear it. First, the one preparing the message needs to know the general characteristics of children: their way of thinking and feeling, the way they learn, what each age level is able to comprehend. Piaget is perhaps the best authority on childhood development, and a pastor would benefit by becoming aware of his work. But for a Christian understanding of the stages of development read *Faith Passages and Patterns* by Thomas A. Droege (Fortress Press, 1983).

While it is important for the preacher of children's messages to be aware of abilities of children at each age of childhood, it is also important to be aware that the children's message is for a wide age range. Preaching a children's message is not like teaching in a single-grade classroom, but like a multigrade room. And there is an advantage in that. All children do not develop at the same rate. The point of a children's message will be above the abilities of some of the hearers. That need not be bad, as long as the child is not tested on understanding or made to feel bad or inadequate. Parents speak to a six-month-old even though they know the child is not yet able to speak back. However, talking to the child will help him or her to reach the level of speech. Young children can be exposed to material beyond their ability, and it will help prepare them for the time when they can understand and apply it.

Likewise, it does not hurt older students to review concepts that are below their ability. Children in multigrade rooms benefit from the review as they listen to the repeat of material they received in lower grades. The same can apply to children's messages.

Second, the preacher needs to be aware of the specific children who will hear the message now being prepared. What is happening in their families? What is worrying them? What has excited them?

Read the text and ask: What would the children ask about this section of Scripture? What ideas in the text would they want to talk about? How long would a child be interested in that subject? What would children add to the subject? How would they change the subject? Remember, if the children won't want to talk about it, they won't want to hear about it either. A good way to evaluate the content of any sermon: instead of seeing the sermon as being spoken from the pulpit to the pew, imagine yourself sitting with the listeners around the table. Would they be interested in the subject of the sermon? What questions would they ask? At what point would they find an excuse to leave the table?

Visit children in their classrooms and playgrounds. Talk to them when you are with them on their home ground—that is, in situations where you need to ask the questions, and they have the answers. Also, invite children to be with you on your home ground—your office or the front of the church. Listen to the questions they ask.

Watch for the emotions that children express. Notice how

fast the emotion can develop and then disappear. Watch how children face new situations. See the things they want to touch. Notice what they react to. For example, while walking across a playground on the first day of a new school year, I heard one five-year-old ask another, "Do you want to be my friend?" On another occasion I was talking to some four-year-olds about their pets. One said she had a cat, so I asked what kind. She said, "It is black and white and dead."

Watch a few children's TV programs. Visit the children's section of a library. Spend some time in a toy shop.

Discover that the world of children is a real world. Many parts of it are the same as when you were a child. You will feel at home with them. But the world of children changes too. If you are to help them see Jesus in their daily lives, you must know what Jesus is doing and what the children are doing. Your sermon brings the actions of Jesus and the children together.

The Objects

Select an object that brings the message of the text and the lives of the children together. "Object," in that sentence, is a pun. It means to select an object—that is, an end toward which the sermon is directed. It also means to select an object—that is, something that is perceived by the senses as a visible or tangible thing.

The object (*goal*) of the object (*thing*) must be clearly defined. An object is not an attention-getter. If a sermon starts with an interesting object, the listeners/viewers will all start paying attention, but if the use of the text and the application is not equally interesting, the attention will be lost. It is better not to get the attention of the hearers at all than to get it and then lose it. If you never get their attention, they may not notice that you had nothing to say. But if you have their attention and then have nothing to give them, the lack of a clear point will be obvious.

The objects that the children see (or hear or smell) must help them understand the object of the sermon. The object must, therefore, be connected with both the text and with the lives of the children. The children must be able to see how the object relates to their lives. Later, when the children hear the text again, it should remind them of the object (and vice versa).

The object should not be something that is complicated and needs explanation—unless, of course, understanding the complexity is the goal of the sermon. Choose items that the children recognize, understand, and see often. Use things the children bring with them to church, things from their classrooms, things that they would like to touch, taste, or smell. All objects should be large enough for adults in the back row to see—unless, of course, the smallness is a part of the point. When using words printed on posters, pictures, or charts, always make them large enough to be easily seen from the farthest part of the nave.

Many texts suggest the object to be used. Read the text by looking only at the nouns. Are any of the nouns suitable objects to be used in the sermon? Then look at the verbs to see what happened to the objects. Could you repeat the same action in the sermon? (See Example 13.) The Bible, especially the Old Testament, uses lots of picture language. If the text talks about weeds, then bring a weed to church. If it talks about salt, bring salt.

As you prepare the message, put the words and the objects together. Each word and each object must have a purpose. Using unnecessary words will distract from the necessary words and blur the meaning of the message. Using unnecessary objects will also obscure the point of the message. Each word and each object is to serve as a clue to help the children understand the text. False or misleading clues will confuse the children.

Objects as Props

The simplest way to use an object in children's message is as a prop for a story. Often the text is from a Bible story. In many other cases a story will help explain the meaning of a text. If the story is about a child going to the library, a book or a library card might make a good prop for the story (Example 34). Using the object helps the child see the story as it happens. In this case, the object is nothing more than a visual background for the story. The object is a secondary teaching method. The primary method is the story itself. The strength of the illustration must, therefore, be in the story, not in the object.

Children love stories, so it is natural to use stories in children's messages (Example 3). The story becomes the object (*thing*) that helps the children understand the object (*goal*) of the message. However, the story, like any visual object, must be related both to the children and to the message. The temptation for the preacher who is a great storyteller is to tell an exciting story that children will remember. But there may be no value in the story other than for entertainment. The temptation for the preacher who is eager to get the spiritual point across is to tell a story that proves the point very well, but is a dull story.

For a story to achieve its purpose, it must seem like a real story to the children. They should be able to identify with the people and the situation in the story. As in any good story, the characters must have names and identity. The plot needs conflict, humor, tension, action, suspense, reality—or at least several of the above.

Find a way to evaluate the use of stories. Would children be interested in the story if it were told apart from the children's message? Would they say, "Tell us another story"? In what way will the story help the children understand, remember, or apply the text?

Objects as Choices

Objects may also be used to offer children a choice (Examples 10, 25, 38). The ability to make decisions is an important part of maturity. Christian commitment, values, and service are based on decision making. Children need to know how one decision is dependent on another. They need an awareness of primary and secondary decision making. For example, our decisions regarding the Christian life are secondary decisions based on the primary decision made by Christ to save us. Children need to have opportunities to make small decisions on their own and to experience the results of those decisions. They also need to know the effects of a decision on the immediate and the distant future. The ability to delay gratification is a sign of maturity. However, a child can begin to learn the concept by making decisions and evaluating the results.

Children need to learn how to make the choice between right and wrong. Such choices may be simple when offered in a church service in the presence of parents and the pastor. However, those choices can cause big problems when made under other circumstances. A children's message can offer the choices to children in an environment where they can make the morally correct choice. Each act of decision making will reinforce their ability to make similar decisions in other circumstances. Sermons that offer moral decisions to children can also include the help of Christ in making the correct decision—and the forgiveness of Christ to those who make the wrong decision. Learning how to make good decisions must also include how to decide what to do after one has made a bad decision. A message that raises the issues of moral choices must always offer God's grace in Christ to those who have made wrong decisions.

The choice of objects also helps children make choices that do not include moral decisions. Since all Christians are not alike, they do not all have the same needs, and they do not all serve Christ in the same way. Objects may be used to help children identify what they need from God. As they make their choices they identify their needs and are reminded of the love and power of God to help fill those needs. Objects may also be used to help children see the many different ways they can serve Christ in their daily lives. As they make their choices, they will recognize the abilities and interests God has created in them. Such decisions can help children recognize God's presence in their lives as they make career and personal decisions for their lives.

Objects as Participation

People are passive when they hear sermons. Their only choice is to agree or disagree. The preacher hopes their agreement or disagreement will be strong enough to change their lives later. However, studies show that sermons are better at reinforcing existing convictions than they are at establishing new action.

Using object lessons can move people one step away from being passive and one step closer to being active. Objects give the hearers an opportunity to become doers (Examples 4, 5, 11). In some cases the doing is a real action that helps the children become doers of the Word right on the spot, instead of hearers only. In other cases the action is a symbolic action that helps the children see what and how they can do the things being suggested in the message. By their symbolic participation they are practicing for real participation in their daily lives.

Objects can be used to show how the people in a Bible story did something. A little boy gave five loaves of bread and two fish to the disciples. The disciples gave the same amounts to Jesus. Jesus gave bread and fish to the disciples. The disciples took the bread and fish from Jesus and fed over 5000 people. By following the objects as they are passed from hand to hand, the children can share in a participation that also involved a child. The children can then participate by giving things they have to Jesus who gives them back to be passed on to others.

Objects as Symbols

The Christian church has a rich heritage of symbolism. Many congregations make good use of symbols in their worship areas. Those symbols are natural objects to be used in children's messages (Examples 17, 18, 24).

The cross, an altar, candles, a baptismal font, flags, windows, vestments, or altar cloths are all natural objects for children's messages. It is very easy for church members to become so accustomed to the decor of their place of worship that they no longer respond to the symbols, which were included for a good reason. An occasional children's message that explains the meaning of a fixture in the church will both teach the children and remind the adults of the point of a worship aid. Once an item in the church has been clearly identified and explained, continued references to it in other sermons keep people aware of its purpose.

Seasonal variations such as banners, changes in altar cloths, Advent wreaths, Christmas trees, or flowers also make good objects for children's messages. Church members sometimes have a difficult time in accepting something new in their area of worship (such as new communion ware, art objects, and the like). If these new items are introduced to the congregation and their purposes are explained, people can more easily accept and understand the change. The children's message offers a good opportunity to explain the changes that are a part of the life of a congregation.

Other symbols that are not a part of the church building can also be used as objects in children's messages. Copies of well-known Christian art often serve as objects to illustrate the message. If your congregation uses a bulletin subscription service that offers a different bulletin cover each Sunday, check the bulletins weeks or months in advance of their use. Some may suggest a good object—one that can be taken home for further use.

The person who preaches children's messages often to the same congregation can also develop symbols that will become known to those who worship regularly. A wrapped gift can become a symbol for grace. A heart can become a symbol for love. A rope that reaches to the cross can be a symbol of faith in Christ. After the symbol has been introduced and explained, whenever it is again referred to or displayed, the worshipers will recall its meaning.

Objects as Illustrations

One of the most obvious uses of objects in sermons is as an illustration (Examples 6, 9, 18). An object that illustrates is meant to say, "This is how it works." The response is to be, "I see."

The object (*thing*) must illustrate the object (*goal*). If the object lesson becomes too complicated, it will conceal the point of the message rather than illuminate it. For the illustration to be clear to the viewers, it must be carefully explained. For example, a ball can be used in a number of ways. If the message includes a story about playing ball, the ball is a prop that helps act out the story. But as an illustration, the ball can visualize a conversation between God and a child. God (who always speaks first) says something to the child (*throw the ball to the child*); the child hears what God says (*the ball is caught*); the child talks to God (*the child throws the ball back*). In this case the ball is not serving as a ball, but as an illustration. It must be explained, so that the viewers see the moving back and forth of the ball in the way a conversation is passed from speaker to hearer and back again. A lesson from experience: the preacher often knows the meaning of the objects being used, but does not always clearly explain the meaning to the hearers. Without a clear explanation of the meaning of the object, the illustration becomes a source of confusion.

Illustrations do not prove a point; they only explain it. The illustration is not to be used as an authority that says something is true because a parallel can be shown. Objects used as illustrations are like parables; they have a point of comparison. Spin-offs beyond the point of comparison can confuse or contradict the message being taught.

All object lessons that depend on actions will sometimes fail. Balloons will break when they are not supposed to—or refuse to break when they should! Anything electrical is subject to whims of an electrical nature. Containers will tip over. Don't let the possibility of objects failing keep you from using them. Words also often fail us by coming out wrong or getting in some perverse order, yet we continue to use words. Therefore we can continue to use objects. If the object (*thing*) fails, be ready to change the object (*goal*) of the sermon to: "This shows that you can't trust anything except Jesus."

People as Objects

People often serve as good objects in a children's message (Examples 1, 7, 40). Include the children, their parents, yourself, and others in the message. Let the children take the part of adults, teachers, and other people in their lives. If it will help the viewers remember whom a child represents, use signs with names or titles.

The Message Is Ready

When you have added a truth from God to the lives of people and have found a way to bring the two together in a way that helps the worshipers learn more about themselves and God, you have a sermon ready to be delivered. But just as the proof of the pudding is in the eating, the proof of a sermon is not in the preparation but in the preaching. That's the next chapter.

Chapter 3

PREACHING THE MESSAGE

As the proof of the pudding is in the eating, the proof of a sermon is in its preaching. A well-prepared sermon must also be well-preached. Delivering a children's sermon includes all of the needs of any other sermon—plus a few more.

Books, discussion, and lectures on preaching assume that the pastor (or one of the pastors) of a congregation will be doing the preaching. Most children's messages used in the regular worship services will also be preached by a pastor, but it need not always be true.

Some pastors cannot sing. Some are not good counselors. None can do everything that is required of the total office of the pastoral ministry. Some pastors are not comfortable preaching children's messages. They may be excellent preachers; they may relate to children well; but they may correctly feel that they do not have the skills needed to have a special sermon for children.

The pastor who does not want to preach children's messages can ask someone else to do it. Immediate candidates are other staff members, such as day school teachers or youth ministers, or lay members, such as Sunday school teachers or others who have special skills and interests in communication with children. In some cases Sunday school classes might take turns in giving the children's message.

Even when the pastor enjoys doing children's messages, there may be advantages in having others in the congregation share in this function. When lay people are involved in leading a worship service, the congregation grows in an appreciation of the priesthood of all believers. Participation in the worship service helps people grow in their understanding of worship and helps them develop God-given abilities. Young people in the congregation who are considering becoming pastors might appreciate the opportunity to preach a children's message as a way of trying out their ability for the office.

Using Prepared Messages

Numerous books of children's messages are available. The person wishing to use children's messages may easily feel that by the purchase of a book all the work of preparation is done; the only job left is the delivery. Not so! While published messages can be a resource to help in the preparation, they cannot replace the work of studying both the text and those who are to hear it. If you prepare your own children's messages, the major work is in the writing. When you use a printed message, the major work is in the adapting and preaching.

Just as it takes skill to prepare a message, it also takes skills to adapt and deliver a published message. Since I have written 15 books of children's messages, people frequently say to me (in an almost apologetic way), "I use your messages, but I always change them a little." My response is, "Great! When I use them in my own congregation, I change them too!" A children's message cannot be delivered by reading from a book held in one hand while holding an object in the other. Do not think of a published message as a meal from a fast-food place—ready to be unwrapped and served. Instead, see it as a cake mix to which more ingredients must be added as it is prepared to be eaten.

First, select books of children's messages to match your need. Read a random sampling of the messages to see if the goals match your own. You can adapt style, objects, and language, but if the book is to help you, it must aim the message in the same direction you aim yours. Some books of children's messages regard all children as non-Christians and aim for conversion; some aim to teach moral living; others aim at teaching doctrine. Some are prepared to be used in worship services; others are aimed at classroom activities. Each may have its purpose. Checking out a variety of books may help you evaluate your own goals in preaching. Then buy the books that help you reach those goals.

When using a published message, let the author's work be a base from which you start your own study, rather than a limitation. The written message may open some doors to help you understand the text. However, your experience may add to that of the author. You may find more doors to be opened. Do not let the printed message stand between you and the text. Instead, use the message as an introduction to the text. Then you will get personally acquainted with what the Scripture says.

Evaluate the story, objects, or means of illustration used by the author. Will those who hear you identify with them? Is there a way to make the story or object more personal for your hearers? Remember, the author had to select items for a general, and unknown, audience; you know exactly to whom you are speaking. Also, the toys and games used by children change from area to area, and most are current for only a short time. Published messages must always use general items; you can be more specific as you adapt the object to your time and place.

Don't be afraid to change a published message to your style and your hearer's needs. If the message you preach is effective, you—not the one who wrote the book—get the credit. If the sermon flops, you—not the one who wrote the book—take the blame.

The 40 sample children's messages included in this book were prepared for a particular audience—a fairly liturgical Lutheran church in Arizona. Naturally they will need to be adapted to other traditions and locations.

The Place of the Children's Message

Where does the children's message belong in the worship service and in the church?

Include the children's message in the worship service in the place where it adds to the development of the theme of the service. Having the children's message before the main sermon gives the preacher the opportunity to use examples from the children's message in the sermon. A natural place for the children's message is after the scripture lessons and before the sermon hymn. If the sermon hymn follows the sermon, the children's message can be immediately before the sermon. It can also be included immediately before the sermon or (if the children are not asked to come to the front) as one of the points in the sermon. Having the children's message midway in the service gives the children an interesting interlude and makes the entire service seem shorter for them.

Most often, children are invited forward for their message. This gives the pastor and children an opportunity to be close together and improves communication. It also gives the children an opportunity to see the church from the front—which they often appreciate. Asking the children to sit in the front often requires the pastor to stand with his or her back to the rest of the congregation. It is better for the pastor to stand to the side, or to have the children sit immediately in front of the pews, so the pastor can still face both the children and the rest of the congregation.

Asking the children to come forward requires someone to identify who is a child. Coming forward for the first time can be a big event for children at the bottom end of the age range. The decision to stop going forward can be one of the signs that the young person has decided he or she is not a child anymore. Usually, if a simple invitation is made for the children to come up for their sermon, the kids and the parents work this out without problems.

In a small worship area, there are advantages in having the children remain seated with parents. It is less disturbing. The pastor can speak to everyone more easily. However, if the pastor is farther away from the last row than the distance for a comfortable conversation (about six pews?), it is better to ask the children to come to the front.

If a children's choir is seated near the front, invite the nonsingers to the area near the choir. That avoids moving a large group. Or if the choir moves to the front to sing, include the children's message immediately after the choir sings.

The First Paragraph

The first paragraph, perhaps the first sentence, is the most important part of a sermon. Do not start with long greetings, discussions about what has been going on in church or community, explanations of the church year, or anything else that has nothing to do with the subject of your sermon. Public speakers are taught to introduce themselves in order to let the audience pick up the ambience of their voice and personality, but a sermon is not an after-dinner speech. The order of worship that has led to the children's sermon has "warmed up" the listeners. The first words spoken should both attract the attention of the worshipers and introduce the subject of the sermon.

Because the first words spoken are important, lead sentences to a sermon have a tendency to get too complicated. For an adult sermon the first sentence should be limited to one comma or semicolon; for a children's sermon, none. If the first sentence gets too complicated, the listener is lost from the beginning. First, let the hearers get the idea of the sermon from you, then lead them with you to more complex ideas. The first sentence needs a strong verb and at least one concrete noun.

Using the Objects

If children's sermons with objects are to be used regularly in a church, certain basic furniture is required. Rather than enduring weekly frustration, get the proper tools.

First, a place is needed to store the objects where they cannot be seen before the sermon. Some pulpits have space for most objects. If a door leads from the front of the church to a side room, install a shelf in that room with a sign: "For object lessons only," so items can be reached easily. Put a box in some convenient but out-of-sight location. Objects need to be stored where they can easily be reached, where efficient worship leaders and ushers will not move them, and where they can be left from one service to the next. The person responsible for bringing the object lessons to the service is also responsible for taking them away. Last week's object lesson is this week's junk—especially to those who do not preach the children's message but who have other responsibilities in the front of the church.

Those who use children's messages regularly also frequently need a small table or flat surface to display the objects. Some churches already have a place that serves well. If nothing is already available, find a small table that can be placed in the front for the entire service. Flower stands sometimes work well. A TV table or end table may be used, though they are often too short. Best of all, make a table that fits your needs. Perhaps such a table can be designed to be a storage place for the objects as well.

Do not show the object until it is needed in the message. The purpose of the object is to attract attention to the subject of the message. Since visuals attract more attention than audio signals, use the visual to enhance the spoken words. After the object has been introduced and used, put it aside. Point to or pick up the object later to remind the viewers of the truth it proclaims. Do not hold the object or move it around when it is not being used to help get the truth across.

If the object used in the children's sermon has some application to the main sermon, it can be left in view for the rest of the service or displayed again during the later sermon.

If the object used in a children's message has some lasting value as a reminder of the point of the message, display it in the church for several Sundays following its use. For example, a picture or other art object used at the beginning of a season might remain on a church bulletin board for the rest of the season. Some objects could be placed on a table or other display area near the entrance of the church. Others can be given to children to take home; by keeping the object in their room they continue to identify with the truth given.

Preparing for the Unexpected

One of the fears that keeps many pastors and teachers from starting to use children's messages is the same joy that makes others keep on using them regularly: when you invite the children forward, you are never sure what is going to happen. Children will give answers that are not expected; they will ask questions that are not relevant to the text, the church year, or anything else on the preacher's agenda.

But the risks are worth it! The preacher's natural desire to keep control of the situation may mean that the truth also remains in the preacher's control. The involvement of the children may mean that they also become involved in the truth.

Face real and potential situations head-on. Every group includes one child who wants your job; he or she will take the sermon away from you every time the opportunity is offered. This is not a problem; it is an opportunity to encourage a young person to become a pastor or other church worker. However, face the situation and do not let it become a problem for other children (who may resent your understudy). If the same child attempts a takeover each week, talk to your "volunteer assistant" prior to the service and ask for his or her cooperation. Offer to answer questions and share ideas after the worship service.

If large numbers of children come forward for the children's message, especially very young ones, you may want to have an adult assistant who helps the children be seated and sits with them to help them participate. The assistant can help prevent behavior problems that might interfere with the message.

The greatest challenge for those who preach children's sermons is to cope with and reply to the variety of questions and responses that children contribute. There is no way to anticipate what a child might say. Their remarks help the preacher understand how they think and what interests them. Often their statements can be incorporated into the planned message. Sometimes what they have to say adds to the message and is of value to others.

Often the children will ask questions or make comments about a subject that have nothing to do with the content of your message. Be happy when children regard the message time as discussion time. It means their minds are involved in the message. They feel a need to ask questions. Answer some questions briefly. Respond to others by telling the questioners that you will talk about it with them later. And remember to keep your promise.

Be careful about the kind of questions you ask in the children's message. Do not ask simplistic questions that are always answered by: (*a*) because Jesus loves me, (*b*) because the Bible says so, or (*c*) both of the above. On the other hand, if your questions are greeted with silence, they are too difficult or too vague. Ask opinion and experience questions: What do you think? What have you done?

Those who use children's messages regularly have many stories of meaningful things that children have contributed to a message that have helped others. I will limit myself to telling one such story here. After a message for children on Easter morning one child asked, "Why did we call it Good Friday, when Jesus had to hurt and die?" I used the question to briefly restate the victory-over-death message of Easter. The next morning the child's mother phoned. She told that after church the family had gone to a restaurant for brunch, where their family of five was seated between two large groups who were giving champagne toasts to one another as part of family celebrations. In a semiquiet moment the child who asked the question raised his glass of milk and said in a loud voice, "I just want to say that I'm glad Jesus rose from the dead." His "Easter sermon" was heard and appreciated by people throughout the restaurant.

The Last Words

Just as the introduction to a message must be well planned, so must the conclusion. A good rule that applies to leading children's games and preaching children's messages: stop while they are still interested. If you feel you haven't got the point across, do not add more explanation. Instead, wind up with a brief reference to the introduction, a last reminder of the object or a short application, and end the message. The final words will not be remembered as well as the first. Do not destroy the good results of the first words by adding too many at the end.

Enjoy This Ministry

No one message for children will include all the ideas and methods mentioned in these chapters. Use those things that help you and the children in your congregation to enjoy the children's message. Help them take home a point in their minds and in their hearts. If you finish a message with a feeling that you are glad you preached it, and you let the children see your joy, they will also be glad they were there. When they leave the worship service, greet them with the same interest, enthusiasm, and respect that you give to adults.

Example 1
Small Children

Who Is the Greatest?

THE WORD

"At that time the disciples came to Jesus, asking, 'Who is the greatest in the Kingdom of heaven?' So Jesus called a child, had him stand in front of them, and said, 'I assure you that unless you change and become like children, you will never enter the Kingdom of heaven. The greatest in the Kingdom of heaven is the one who humbles himself and becomes like this child.' " (Matthew 18:1-4).

THE WORLD

An adult, a child, and two chairs.

I have two chairs here in the front. I'm going to ask an adult to sit in one. Mrs. Ludwig (*call an adult by name*), will you sit here? And I want a child to sit in the other. Jennifer (*call a child by name*), will you sit here?

Now I have a question for the rest of you. Which of these two is the greater? Mrs. Ludwig is larger than Jennifer. Mrs. Ludwig makes more money. Mrs. Ludwig knows more than Jennifer. Mrs. Ludwig has been to more places than Jennifer. It sounds like Mrs. Ludwig is the greater.

But before we decide that, let's hear what Jesus said when his disciples asked him who was the greatest. (*Read the text.*)

Does that surprise you? We often tell children to act like adults. Children like to pretend they are grown-ups and dress in their mother's and father's clothes. But Jesus said that adults should become like children; he does not tell the children to become like adults.

You children know that adults have something to give to you. What do adults give you? (*Talk about food, clothing, education, house, etc.*) Adults tell you that Jesus is your friend. They help you know that he is your Savior. Adults have a lot to give to you.

But do you know that you also have something you can give to adults? What do you think you can give to big people? (*Help the children talk about love, smiles, fun, hugs, etc.*) Children add joy and happiness to the lives of adults.

Jesus mentions something very special that children have and that adults need. He says that adults must be humble like a child. A humble person does not think he or she is better than others. A humble person is willing to receive help from others. A humble person is not proud. Jesus says that adults can learn to be humble from children.

As you children grow up, you will become adults. But you can always remember what it is like to be a child. Enjoy being a child now. When you are an adult, you will remember the fun you had when you were little. When you are an adult, you can keep all the good things about being a child.

Thank you for helping me, Mrs. Ludwig and Jennifer. Both of them, and all of us, are great in the kingdom of God, because we are all the children of God. Jesus has made all of us the children of God, because he takes us to be with God.

Example 2
Small Children

Look at What You Are Wearing

THE WORD

"You were baptized into union with Christ, and now you are clothed, so to speak, with the life of Christ himself" (Galatians 3:27).

THE WORLD

You prepare for this sermon as you dress in the morning. Wear a shirt or blouse that can be destroyed. If that is not practical, use colored chalk to mark your clothing instead of tearing it as indicated in the sermon below. You will also need a jacket or sweater to put on later in the sermon.

Do you notice what I wear when I talk to you about Jesus? See what I have on now. You wouldn't have remembered what I am wearing, if I hadn't mentioned it. But suppose I had an accident right before I came to church. Suppose I tore my shirt [blouse] like this. (*Tear a hole in the garment in a place that would be covered by a jacket, or make a blotch on the garment with the chalk.*)

Now you would remember what I am wearing. I would be embarrassed if I had a hole in my shirt while I was here with you. I would probably try to hide the hole by putting my hand over it. (*Cover hole with hand.*) Or I would try to stand so that you couldn't see the hole. (*Do so.*) But you would still see the hole. In fact, as I tried to hide it, you would see that something was wrong. Then you would be sure to see the hole.

In some ways this hole in my shirt is like sin. We sin when we say or do something wrong. Our sins make us look bad, as this hole makes my shirt look bad. We are embarrassed by our sin, and we try to hide it. But when we try to hide our sin, other people see it anyway. Sin ruins our lives, just as this hole ruined my shirt.

The Bible tells us we do not have to hide our sin. Jesus knows that we have sinned. He has done something to help us. Listen to this: "You were baptized into union with Christ, and now you are clothed, so to speak, with the life of Christ himself."

You were "baptized into union with Christ." That means you belong to him. You and Jesus are together. You are "clothed in the life of Christ." That means you get to wear the gifts that Jesus gives to you.

See this jacket. Pretend it is the life of Christ. The jacket is what Jesus gave me when he died on the cross. The jacket is what Jesus gave me when he rose from the dead. Look what happens when I put the jacket on. *(Put on jacket.)* Can you see the hole now? The jacket covers the hole. Now I don't have to hide it. I am not embarrassed because you cannot see the hole.

Because you are baptized in Jesus' name, you are also clothed in Christ. That means you wear Jesus. Jesus is like this jacket. He covers your sin. He takes away all the bad things you have done. You do not have to hide the wrong things.

You know I still have a hole in my shirt, even though the jacket covers it. But when Jesus covers our sins, the sins are gone. He took them away by dying for us. You can wear Jesus all your life and always be forgiven.

Example 3
Sermon on context of Romans 14:5-9
Story

Whose Opinion Is Important?

THE WORD

"Who are you to judge the servant of someone else? It is his own Master who will decide whether he succeeds or fails. And he will succeed, because the Lord is able to make him succeed" (Romans 14:4).

THE WORLD

A child's drawing of himself or herself leading a dog.

Mark went to a Christian day school. His teacher gave the class an art assignment. Each student had to draw a picture showing how he or she had done something to serve Jesus. When Mark was doing his homework, he drew this picture. *(Show picture.)*

What do you see? This is Mark. This is a dog, but it is not Mark's dog. The dog belongs to his neighbor. She was sick and could not walk her dog. So Mark took her dog for a walk every afternoon. He liked to help his neighbor, and he remembered that Jesus said to help other people. Mark liked his picture.

When Mark's older brother saw the picture, he laughed. He said the dog looked more like a sheep. That made Mark feel bad, so he showed the picture to his mother. His mother said that if the picture was to show how he served Jesus, he should have drawn a picture of a church and a cross. Mark did not like his picture anymore, but he didn't have time to draw another.

The next day Mark felt bad when he put the picture on his teacher's desk. He thought he would get a bad grade. But when the teacher asked him to explain the picture to the rest of the class, he felt better. The teacher said it was a good picture. She put it on the bulletin board for everyone to see.

Mark's brother didn't like the picture. His mother didn't like the picture. But the teacher did. Whose opinion was more important? Mark's mother and brother had not given the assignment. They would not give Mark his grade. It was more important that the teacher liked the picture.

Sometimes we judge others and make them feel bad. Sometimes others judge us and make us feel bad. We have to remember whose judgment or opinion is important. Listen to what Paul tells us: "Who are you to judge the servant [we could say *student*] of someone else? It is his own Master [we could say *teacher*] who will decide whether he succeeds or fails. And he will succeed because the Lord is able to make him succeed."

In the story I told, the teacher gave the assignment, so the teacher gave the grade. Jesus is the one who has told us how to live with him. Therefore, Jesus is the one to judge us. We are not to judge others or worry when others judge us.

When we do fail at something, we know Jesus will forgive us, because he is the Savior who died to pay for our sins. Remember, when Paul told us that Jesus is our Master who will judge us, he also said, "And he will succeed, because the Lord is able to make him succeed." You can serve God. You can do what is right. You can, because Jesus is on your side. He is able to forgive you. He is also able to make you succeed.

Be glad that Jesus is the one who judges you, because he loves and helps you. Remember, he loves and helps others too, so you need not judge them.

Example 4
Participation

All Sinners Get in Line

THE WORD
"Christ was without sin, but for our sake God made him share our sin in order that in union with him we might share the righteousness of God" (2 Corinthians 5:21).

THE WORLD
An envelope for each child, a cross, and a roll of tape.

I'm going to give each of you an envelope. Pretend that your envelope has a list of all your sins in it. The list of your sins is in an envelope, so no one knows what it says but you. You know what you have done wrong. You know the things you have said that are wrong. Pretend that all those things are on the list I am giving you.

But I am not going to give Kellie *(call one child by name)* an envelope. Let's pretend she represents Jesus. Since Jesus did not sin, he would not have a list of sins. Instead, he had a cross. So I will give Kellie this cross. Remember this is Jesus with the cross. The rest of you have a list of your sins.

Now listen to what the Bible says, "Christ was without sin, but for our sake God made him share our sin in order that in union with him we might share the righteousness of God."

Let me show you how this works. I want all those who have sins to stand in line in front of me. This line is for those who have sinned and must pay for their sins. Bring your envelopes with you and get in line. *(Help the children get in line.)*

What about Jesus? Does he belong in this line? He has no sin. But remember, the Bible says that for our sake Jesus shared in our sin. He stood in line with us. *(Put the person with the cross about third in line.)* We have our sins, but look what Jesus has. See the cross.

(Speak to the first person.) You are here to pay for your sins. The price of sin is death. Can you pay that? Then you stand aside. *(Do the same with several more children. Then speak to the child who represents Jesus.)* Now Jesus is next in line. You have no sin, Jesus. You don't belong in this line.

Remember, Jesus shares in our sin in order to give us his righteousness. He didn't stand in line to pay for *his* sins. He stood in line to pay for ours. He died for us. He takes all our sins on himself. *(Have each child tape his or her envelope to the cross.)* We give our sins to Jesus. He died for us. He has paid the price of our sin.

When we come to church, we confess our sins. That means you admit your sins to God. Imagine that you are putting your sins in an envelope and giving them to Jesus. Jesus is here too. He is here to take away our sins and to give us his goodness. When you leave today, you will leave your sins on the cross. You take the love of Jesus with you instead.

Example 5
Participation
Sense of Taste

Every Grape Was Sour

THE WORD

"My friend had a vineyard on a very fertile hill. He dug the soil and cleared it of stones; he planted the finest vines. He built a tower to guard them, dug a pit for treading the grapes. He waited for the grapes to ripen, but every grape was sour" (Isaiah 5:1b-2).

THE WORLD

Grapes for each child.

I want to read a song to you from Isaiah, a prophet in the Old Testament. It is: "My friend had a vineyard on a very fertile hill. He dug the soil and cleared it of stones; he planted the finest vines. He built a tower to guard them, dug a pit for treading the grapes. He waited for the grapes to ripen, but every grape was sour."

This farmer worked very hard. Let's help him. First he had to dig the field. Come, let's dig. (*Ask all the children to pretend to dig.*) See those big rocks. We'll have to pile them over there. (*Have the children pretend they are carrying rocks from the field.*) This is hard work. It is hot here.

Now we have the field all dug. We must plant the vines. Dig some holes in the ground. Put the plants in the soil. We are working hard. Are your hands sore? Does your back hurt?

Now we have to wait for the vines to grow, but we must protect them. We'll build a tower so a guard can watch our field and protect it. Come on, help me build the tower. Now, that's finished, but you still can't rest. We must guard our plants.

Now the grapes are ripe. We have worked hard to get these grapes. Now we can enjoy the grapes. Let's all pick some. *(Pretend to do it.)* Are you ready to eat the grapes? *(Pretend to do it.)* Ooh! They are sour. They don't taste good. We did all that hard work. We got sores on our hands. We were hot. Look what we got—sour grapes.

Isaiah told that story to show us how God feels when we sin. God created a beautiful world and worked hard to make a good place for us to live. Just as a farmer plants vines in order to have good grapes, God created us to have happy people. But the farmer got sour grapes, and God had people who were like sour grapes. We get angry and say bad things. We tell lies. We hurt each other. We forget God. We are like sour grapes in God's mouth.

But that's not the end of the story. We were like sour grapes, but God sent Jesus to change us. Jesus is our Savior who takes our sin away. God the Father worked to create the world and all that is in it. Jesus added his work to the work his Father had done. Jesus died for us. He changed us from sour grapes to sweet grapes.

I brought each of you some good grapes. *(Distribute them.)* Taste these. Aren't they good? Because Jesus is your Savior, you do not taste like sour grapes to God. Instead, you are like these good grapes. When you say or do something bad, re-member the story of the sour grapes. Ask Jesus to forgive you. Then you will not be like a sour grape.

Example 6
Decision
Illustration

What Do You Think?

THE WORD

"[Jesus said,] 'What about you? . . . Who do you say I am?' "
(Matthew 16:15).

"[Jesus said,] 'What do you think a man does who has one
hundred sheep and one of them gets lost?' " (Matthew 18:12).

"[Jesus said,] 'Now, what do you think?' " (Matthew 21:28).

"[Jesus said,] 'Tell us, then, what do you think?' " (Matthew
22:17).

THE WORLD

A small box with a button in it, a shoe box with a teddy
bear in it, a long mailing tube with both ends closed, a large
flat box, another small box.

Jesus was a teacher. His disciples were his students. He taught
them many things. He taught them about the kingdom of
God, about forgiveness. He taught them about his death and
resurrection.

Jesus wanted his disciples to learn. He also wanted them to
think. Listen to what he said to his disciples. (*Read the above
texts from a Bible and mention where each section is located.*)
Earlier in his life Jesus taught the disciples. When he was close
to his death, he wanted to see if the disciples had learned

what he had taught. He asked for their opinion. He wanted to know if they could think.

Let me show you the difference between learning and thinking. First I will teach you something. A button is in this box. *(Take the button out and show it. Put it back.)* You learned what I showed you and told you. What is in this box? *(Hold up the same box.)* A button. That's right! You learned.

Now I want you to think. A teddy bear is in one of these boxes. I'm not going to tell you which one. You think about it. Which box contains the teddy bear? *(When they pick the right box, say:)* How did you know it was in the shoe box? You knew it couldn't be in the small box. But these *(hold up the tube and the flat box)* are also large, but they were not the right shape. You could think and know which box contained the teddy bear.

Now let's talk about learning and thinking about Jesus. You have learned many things about Jesus. You have learned that he is both God and human. He died to take away your sins. He rose from the dead and still lives. You have been taught those things, and you have learned them.

Now what do you think about Jesus? Suppose you do something wrong? What do you think Jesus does? Suppose someone else does something wrong? What do you think Jesus does? Suppose you are lonely? What does Jesus do? Suppose you are afraid? What does Jesus do?

Jesus taught his disciples. He taught them to think. Jesus also wants you to think. Remember the things you know about Jesus. Then think about what that means in your life.

Example 7
Little Children
Friendship

Jesus Is Your Friend

THE WORD
"[Jesus said,] 'The greatest love a person can have for his friends is to give his life for them. And you are my friends if you do what I command you.' " (John 15:13-14).

THE WORLD
A child.

Do you have a brother or sister? What are their names? Do you know what your father's name is? What is your mother's name? Tell me the names of your friends. (*As the children give names, they may mention Jesus. If so, say,* "That's right. Jesus is your friend," *and read the text. If they name other friends, talk briefly about their friends and say,* "You can have many friends. I want to remind you of one more." *Then read the text.*)

Jesus is your friend. That means he likes to be with you. It means he wants to listen to what you have to say. It also means he wants to talk to you.

A friend helps you when you need help. Jesus is our best friend because he can help us with our most important needs. Some friends help us have fun. Some friends help us when we have work to do. Some friends help us when we are sad or lonely. Jesus is a friend who helps in all of those needs.

But Jesus gives some help that no other friend can give. He says, "The greatest love a person can have for his friends is to give his life for them." Jesus gave his life for us when he died to pay for our sins. First, he gave his life for us. Then he rose from the dead and showed us that he will raise us from the dead too. Jesus is our best friend.

Tara (*call one child by name*), please come up here and stand beside me. Can you pretend that I am Jesus? I am your friend and I stand beside you. Each of you pretend you are standing with Jesus. Because Jesus is your friend, he would put his hand on your shoulder like this. Jesus is your friend and wants to be near you.

Each of you pretend Jesus is with you and has his hand on your shoulder like this. Now think about the worst things you have said and done. Think about the things you said when you were angry. Think about the things you did that no one else knows. If Jesus is with you, he hears and knows those things.

When Jesus knows about the bad things you have done, do you think he pulls his hand away? (*Pull your hand away.*) Or do you think that he hugs you even more? (*Put your arm around the child.*)

Sometimes our other friends leave us when we do something wrong. But Jesus does not leave us when we do wrong. Instead, he forgives us. When we do wrong, we need him even more, because he is the one who died to pay for our sin.

When you do wrong, Jesus does not pull away from you. And you don't have to run away from Jesus either. When you do wrong, you need Jesus all the more. He is the one who forgives you. He is the one who helps you not to do it again.

Remember, Jesus is always your friend. He likes to be with you. He wants you to enjoy being with him.

Example 8
Fear of Death

The Danger of Death

THE WORD

"The danger of death was all around me;
the horrors of the grave closed in on me;
I was filled with fear and anxiety.
Then I called to the Lord,
'I beg you, Lord, save me!' " (Psalm 116:3-4).

THE WORLD

A long rope.

Tell the children about the power lines that are near you. If there is a window, ask the children to look outside at the lines.) Do you know those lines are carrying electricity? What would happen to you if you touched one of those lines? Yes, you could be killed by the electricity in those lines.

Are you afraid of those lines? Are they dangerous to us now? No, because they are far away. They are high so we cannot accidentally touch them. We are safe.

Pretend this rope is one of those electrical lines. You must pretend, because a rope does not really carry electricity. I do not want to scare you with a real wire. Now I want you to think how you would feel if an electrical wire were as close as this. *(Stand about 10 feet away.)* Would you be scared if the wire were this close? *(Move to about 5 feet away.)*

Would you be scared if the rope were very close? *(Hold the rope around,. but not touching, a child.)* Think how careful you would have to be if you were this close to an electrical wire.

Think of that wire out there, and this rope here, as death. We are not afraid of death when it seems far away. But when death is close to us, it scares us. The person who wrote Psalm 116 felt that death was near him. He said, "The danger of death was all around me; the horrors of the grave closed in on me; I was filled with fear and anxiety."

We don't think about death often, because it seems far away. But even when it is far away, some people worry about dying. I may think that someone in my family will die. Or I might think I will die. That could worry me.

I want to talk to you about how people feel when the danger of death seems close, so that you know what to do if you find yourself worrying about dying. This psalm gives us two good points. First, the person who wrote the psalm could admit he was scared and anxious. All of us are scared and anxious when we do something we have never done before. He had never died before, so he wondered what would happen. We do not have to pretend that we are not scared about dying.

The second good point in the psalm is that the man knew God was with him. He called to God and said, "I beg you, Lord, save me!" If you think death is close to you or someone you love, ask God to help you. Many times people are close to death and do not die. They get well again.

But we all will die sometime. God helps us even when we do die. We have never died before. But Jesus, God's Son, has died. Three days after he died, he rose from the dead and is still alive. Because he took away our punishment, we will also be raised from the dead. When death seems close to you, remember that God is even closer. Death will not destroy you. God will protect you.

Example 9
Friendship
Illustration

We Can Be Friends

THE WORD
  "We were God's enemies, but he made us his friends through the death of his Son. Now that we are God's friends, how much more will we be saved by Christ's life! But that is not all; we rejoice because of what God has done through our Lord Jesus Christ who has now made us God's friends" (Romans 5:10-11).

THE WORLD
  Six raw eggs, a box large enough to hold the eggs, and a pack of dinner napkins.

These eggs are raw. I'm going to put all six of the raw eggs into this box. What do you think would happen if I shook the box. *(Hold the box as if you were going to shake it.)* That would make a mess, wouldn't it? The eggs would bump into each other. They would break each other. What a mess!

In some ways each of us is like one of these eggs. The egg has a thin, hard shell that is easily cracked and broken. Each of us has an ego that is easily cracked and broken. Our bodies feel the pain if we are sick or if someone hits us. Our egos are hurt if someone says something bad about us, or lies to us, or says anything that makes us feel bad about ourselves.

When we live with each other in a family or in a class at school, we are like eggs in a box. We bump into each other and hurt each other. Think about what other people have said and done that has hurt you and made you feel bad. Have you said and done things that have hurt other people and made them feel bad? In our family and with our friends we are like eggs in a box. When someone shakes the box, we break each other's egos.

But God has done something to help us. Listen to what Paul tells us in Romans 5. *(Read the text.)*

Our egos are like shells on an egg because they protect us from being hurt. But they also keep us away from one another, so that we cannot enjoy one another. But God sent Jesus to help us. Jesus took away our sin when he died for us. We don't have to protect ourselves anymore, because Jesus protects us. We are wrapped in his love and forgiveness. *(As you talk, wrap each egg in several thicknesses of napkin. Put the eggs in the box. Use enough napkins so the eggs cannot move around.)*

Jesus has removed our sin and made each of us to be God's friend. When we are all God's friends, we can also be each other's friends. None of us need to say or do things that will hurt others. Because we are protected by Jesus, we are not hurt by the things others say or do.

Look what happens when I shake the box now. *(Shake the box.)* The eggs do not break one another. Each is wrapped in a thick covering and is protected from the others. When Jesus is with you in your family or in your classroom, he also protects you from others and others from you. He has taken away our sins so that we can be friends with God and friends with one another.

If you get hurt when you bump into others, or they bump into you, remember what Jesus has done for you. You do not have to go off by yourself to protect yourself. Instead, you have a friend who protects you. When Jesus is with you and others, you can all be friends.

Example 10
Christian Life
Illustration

Be Filled with Something Good

THE WORD
"Fill your minds with those things that are good and that deserve praise: things that are true, noble, right, pure, lovely, and honorable" (Philippians 4:8).

THE WORLD
An attractive bowl, some junk items (torn envelopes, chewing gum wrappers, peanut shells, etc.), and enough fruit to fill the bowl.

Someone gave the Carter family this beautiful bowl. Mrs Carter liked it and wanted the rest of the family and their guests to enjoy it. She put it on the table so that everyone could see it.

But people kept throwing junk in it. Mr. Carter opened the mail and put a torn envelope in the bowl. *(Put envelope in bowl.)* The children in the family threw chewing gum wrappers and peanut shells in it. *(Put other junk items in bowl.)* One guest even put cigarette ashes in the beautiful bowl. The bowl wasn't pretty with all the junk in it.

Mrs. Carter emptied all the rubbish out and was going to put the bowl away in a cabinet to keep it clean. Then she had an idea: she put the bowl back on the table and filled it with fruit. *(Fill bowl with fruit.)* The pieces of fruit were pretty and made the bowl look even better. When the fruit was in the bowl, no one threw junk in it.

Now I want each of you to think of this bowl as if it were your mind. *(Empty the bowl.)* Your mind is beautiful and good. God created your mind so you could have a good life. But sometimes your mind gets filled with junk. *(Put some of the junk items back in the bowl.)*

Can you think of some things that are like junk in your mind? Dirty words are like junk. Names that we call others to hurt them are like junk. Hatred, lies, jealousy, greed, and selfishness are like junk. Things that hurt us are junk in our minds. God did not give us our minds to think of evil and bad things.

But we are all sinners, and we all think of bad things. So God sent Jesus to be our Savior. He forgives our sins. *(Dump the rubbish out of the bowl.)* Jesus takes our sin away.

But God does more than take away our sin. He also sends his Holy Spirit to fill our minds with good things. Listen to what Paul tells us in Philippians 4. *(Read the text.)*

When your mind is filled with good things, there will be no room for the junk that hurts you. When you read the Bible and worship God, your mind is filled with good things. When you have fun that helps you and others, your mind is filled with good things. When you watch television programs that help you learn about life and enjoy it, your mind is filled with good things.

Use your mind to think about what goes into your mind. Think of it as a bowl. Who puts things in your mind? Remember, Jesus helps dump out the junk things. Also remember that the Holy Spirit is there to fill your mind with good things.

Example 11
Evangelism

Who Will Be Our Messenger?

THE WORD
"Then I heard the Lord say, 'Whom shall I send? Who will be our messenger?'

"I answered, 'I will go! Send me!' " (Isaiah 6:8).

THE WORLD
A small cross that can be given away. Also arrange for a person to be available outside the worship area.

I need someone to help me. Who will be my helper? I'm glad so many of you are willing to help. You may put your hands down now. I will choose one of you in a little while. But first I must tell you what kind of help I need.

The Bible reading for today says, "Then I heard the Lord say, 'Whom shall I send? Who will be our messenger?' " God had a job to do. He needed a message delivered. So he asked, "Whom shall I send?" God asked for someone to help him, just as I asked if one of you would help me.

When Isaiah heard God ask for help, he held up his hand. He said, "I will go! Send me!" Isaiah was eager to help God. He wanted to deliver God's message.

I also need one of you to deliver a message for me. This is the message. *(Show the cross.)* Do you know what the cross means? Yes, it means that Jesus loves us. When we see the cross, we remember that he loves us so much that he died for us. He gave his life to pay for our sins. He was punished in our place. Then he rose from the dead. Now he lives with us and promises to take us to heaven.

Do each of you know that message? Do you know Jesus loves you? Can you tell someone else about Jesus' love? Who will be my messenger? I'm glad so many of you are willing to help. I will choose Chad (*call some child by name*).

Chad, will you come and get this cross? Do you remember the message that goes with it? Your job is to go and find someone and give that person the cross. Then tell him or her what the cross means. Then bring the person back here with you. Can you do that?

While Chad is giving our message to someone, let's talk about what he is doing. He is giving a message from God. The message also comes from us. We know God loves us. We know about Jesus. Remember how many of you offered to deliver the message. I picked Chad to do the job for all of us. We often send missionaries to tell others about Jesus. They are taking God's message to other people. When we send the missionaries, they are delivering our message, just as Chad is now doing.

We also ask pastors and teachers to be God's messengers. They tell others the message of Jesus for all of us. But each of you can also be the messenger. You can tell others about Jesus just like Chad is now doing. (*If you are still waiting for the messenger to return, review the message. Ask the children to name people they would have chosen to receive the message. If time requires, ask several to tell something about Jesus.*)

Here is Chad now. What did you tell the person? Did you give the person the cross? You were a good messenger, Chad.

Example 12
Small Children
Education

Now You Know

THE WORD

"In the past I knew only what others had told me, but now I have seen you with my own eyes" (Job 42:5).

THE WORLD

If near Christmas or Easter, several sheets of seals appropriate for the season and an envelope. At another time of the year, a picture of a teacher, a report card, or another item may be substituted for the seals.

Job was a very rich man who became poor and sick. His friends thought God had punished him by taking away his money and his health. But Job knew God was not punishing him. He knew God loved him. Then Job got well. He became rich again. Job learned a big lesson from what happened to him. He said, "In the past I knew only what others had told me, but now I have seen you with my own eyes."

Job always knew about God. His parents had taught him when he was small. His teachers told him about God. He knew about God because he had been taught.

After he had been sick and poor, he learned more about God. He learned not because someone else had taught him, but because he had seen for himself what God had done.

Let me show you how you can learn from others—and then how you learn for yourself. See this envelope. Do you know what is in it? I will teach you. Easter seals are in the envelope. I have taught you something. What is in the envelope? That's right: Easter seals. You know because I taught you.

Watch this. *(Take the seals out of the envelope and show them to the children.)* Now you know because you have seen the seals for yourselves. First you knew because I taught you; then you knew because you saw the seals.

Each time you come to worship, you learn about Jesus. I teach you what Jesus has done for you. *(Name others who also teach the children.)* We teach you that Jesus loves you. We teach you that he died to pay for your sins, and that he rose from the dead to make a place for you in heaven. You know those things because we taught you.

You are like Job. You know about God. But also like Job you can learn more. You can learn for yourself that God is with you. You can be happy because your sins are forgiven. You can trust him and ask him to help you. You can forgive others because he has forgiven you. You learn more about Jesus when you do the things your teachers have taught you.

Now you know about Jesus. You know because I have taught you. But you also know Jesus because he is with you.

(If you have used seals, conclude by explaining the symbol on the seals as it applies to the gospel of Christ, and give each child one of the seals.)

Example 13
Stewardship

When You Give to God

THE WORD
"If the first piece of bread is given to God, then the whole loaf is his also; and if the roots of a tree are offered to God, the branches are his also" (Romans 11:16).

THE WORLD
A loaf of sliced bread, a potted plant, ten dollars (five single dollars and one five-dollar bill), and a child.

Today's Bible verse tells us what happens when we give something to God. The first part of it says, "If the first piece of bread is given to God, then the whole loaf is his also." Here is a loaf of bread. I'll open it and take out one slice and give it to God. *(If you are in a worship area, place the slice of bread on the altar. Otherwise, explain you are giving it to God in another way.)* Giving the bread to God might mean giving it to someone else who also needs something to eat.

Our Bible verse says that the rest of the bread is now God's also. If I use these two pieces *(take a second slice)* to make a peanut butter sandwich, I will remember the first piece went to God. This piece also is God's. I can eat it, because God also wants me to eat. Each piece of bread that I eat will remind me of God because I gave the first slice to him.

What our Bible verse says about bread can also apply to other things. I have ten dollars. *(Show the money.)* I will give one dollar to God. *(Place one dollar on the altar or in an offering plate.)* Now I can spend the other money. But when I spend the other nine dollars, I remember the dollar I gave to God. I spend some money to have fun, and I remember God wants me to enjoy life. I spend some money on food, and I remember God wants me to eat. I spend some money on clothes, and I remember God helps clothe me. When I give the first dollar to God, I remember God when I spend the other nine dollars.

Our Bible verse tells us more about giving to God. It says, "And if the roots of a tree are offered to God, the branches are his also." I couldn't bring a tree in here, so I brought this potted plant. If I want to give the part you can see—these pretty leaves and flowers—I also have to give the roots that you cannot see. *(Place the plant on the altar.)*

Let me show you how that works in our lives. Billy *(speak to a person a distance from you)*, give me your hand. *(As he moves toward you, say:)* No, not all of you. Just your hand, Billy. But that wouldn't work, would it? If I take Billy's hand *(do so)*, I also receive the rest of Billy. *(Put your arm around him.)*

We cannot give only a part of our lives to Jesus. We can't give him only our hearts, or only our minds, or only our hands. If we give a part of ourselves to Jesus, he gets all of us.

When we give a part of anything to God, God gets it all. That is true because God gave himself totally to us. When Jesus came to be God living with us, he did not give us just a part of his life. He gave his whole life for us by dying to pay for our sins. When he rose from the dead, he gave us a way to live again. Jesus did not save only a part of our life. He saved each of us totally. When we give to him we do not give just a part of our life. We give all of our life to him.

LUTHERAN BROTHERHOOD
• A Family of Financial Services for Lutherans

10/17

Example 14
Helping Others
Participation

Pass the Bowl

THE WORD

"Set aside a tithe—a tenth of all that your fields produce each year. Then go to the one place where the Lord your God has chosen to be worshiped; and there in his presence eat the tithes of your grain, wine, and olive oil, and the first-born of your cattle and sheep. Do this so that you may learn to honor the Lord your God always" (Deuteronomy 14:22-23).

THE WORLD

Enough peanuts in the shell so each child may have from two to a handful, an offering plate, and a serving dish.

God gave his people in the Old Testament a special way to give gifts to him. Let me read it to you. *(Read the text.)*

The people were farmers and grew crops. He asked them to give him a tenth of all they grew. That means if they grew 10 bushels of grain, they would give God one bushel. If they raised 100 lambs, they would give God 10 lambs.

I am giving each of you some peanuts. Pretend that you have a garden and that you have grown peanuts. The ones you have now are just one-tenth of your crop. Some of you have more because you grew more. Each is bringing one out of every 10 you grew. You are going to give it to the Lord. *(Pass the offering plate and ask them to put the peanuts in it.)*

Now watch what God did with this offering. (*Pour the pea-nuts from the offering plate into a serving dish. Pass the dish and invite each child to take some peanuts.*) God asked the people to give him a gift; then he gave it back to them. God wanted them to eat what they had raised. You may take the peanuts home and eat them.

But I also want you to take a lesson home with you. Re-member that God gives you all you have. God asks you to give to him; then he gives back to you.

You might wonder why you didn't just keep the peanuts you had in the first place. Here's why. First, God wants you to worship him. The people brought their offerings to the place of worship, just as you came to a place of worship today. God also wanted the people to be together. He wanted them to enjoy one another. They came together to give their offerings to him. Then God gave the food back so that they could be together as they ate it.

Later, God himself came to be with people. Jesus is God who became a person. Jesus gave himself for us when he died for our sins. He gives us love, joy, forgiveness, and many other gifts. Now we can give gifts of love and joy back to him when we worship him.

God wants us to be with him. He also wants us to be with one another. We come together to worship God. We are to-gether with him. God gives us many blessings so that we can share them with one another. In fact, you might find someone to share your peanuts with. When you share the peanuts, also share God's love.

Example 15
World Hunger
Participation

Pass the Bowl around the World

THE WORD
"If the place of worship is too far from your home for you to carry there the tithe of the produce that the Lord has blessed you with, then do this: Sell your produce and take the money with you to the one place of worship. Spend it on whatever you want—beef, lamb, wine, beer—and there, in the presence of the Lord your God, you and your families are to eat and enjoy yourselves" (Deuteronomy 14:24-26).

THE WORLD
A serving dish filled with peanuts, an empty serving dish, an offering plate, money (coins and bills).

God gives us gifts so we can share with one another. These peanuts are food that God has given. We can pass the bowl so that we can all share the food we have from God. But we can pass the bowl only to those who are near us.

Look at the bowl. *(Have the empty bowl in a far corner of the room or, if possible, outside a window.)* It is empty.

We can share the food we have with our family and with people in our community, but some hungry people live a long way from us, some far across the world. We cannot give our food to them; we are too far away to hand it to them. But the Bible tells us of a way to share food with people far away. *(Read the text.)*

If the people lived far from the place of worship, they could sell the things they grew on their farm. Then they could take the money to the place of worship and buy food there to share with others.

You cannot share your lunch or other food with people who live far away. But you can take the money you would use to buy food and give it to a relief agency that helps hungry people. Instead of putting food in our offering plate, we can put money in it. (*Put coins and bills in the offering plate.*)

The people who work for the relief agency can take the money to the place where people are hungry. (*Ask one child to take the bowl of peanuts and stand near the empty bowl. Ask another child to take the money to the first child. The second "buys" the peanuts and puts them in the empty bowl.*)

Jesus has asked us to feed hungry people. Sometimes you can give food to someone who needs it; sometimes you can give money so that someone else can provide food for hungry people. (*Name local and international relief agencies supported by the congregation.*)

We often talk about the great things Jesus has done for us. He died to forgive our sins. He rose from the dead to give us eternal life. But he also cares about our life here on earth. He fed hungry people, and he asks us to do the same. He helped sick people, and he asks us to do the same. He helped lonely people, and he asks us to do the same.

Watch for ways to help people. Sometimes you can help them by yourself; sometimes you can work with others to help many people.

Example 16
Worship

Think about What You Are Doing

THE WORD

"The Lord said, 'These people claim to worship me, but their words are meaningless, and their hearts are somewhere else. Their religion is nothing but human rules and traditions, which they have simply memorized' " (Isaiah 29:13).

THE WORLD

An organ (or piano, if more practical).

We are here to worship Jesus. You worship Jesus when you love him, honor him, praise him, serve him. You worship Jesus when you show him and others that he has first place in your life.

We use many ways to worship Jesus. Often we sing to worship him. We sing songs that talk about Jesus. Let's worship him now by singing. *(Select a song that speaks clearly of Jesus, one that is well known by the children).*

You know the words of the song. Think about what they say. *(Mention thoughts from the song that show worship.)* The song not only has words; it also has a tune. We will ask the organist to play a little bit of it for us. *(Listen to the tune.)* When you hear that tune, it makes you think of the words. Now let's put the words and the music together and sing the song as a way of worshiping Jesus.

That is a good way to worship. However, the Bible reading for today tells us that sometimes we can use words and not mean them. *(Read the text.)*

When God says our hearts may be somewhere else, he means we care about something else. If we speak words that worship Jesus, but we are caring about something else, our words are meaningless. They do not worship Jesus. Sometimes we memorize words and say them without meaning them. That is not worship. Thinking about other things keeps us from thinking about Jesus.

Let me show you how this works. We are going to sing the same song again. I want you to sing it as you did before. The last time the organist helped you by playing the music that helped you think of the words. This time she will not help you. *(Ask the organist to play a tune that the children to do not know—one that is very different from the song the children are singing. Then ask the children to sing the song they sang before.)*

See how difficult that was. You were trying to sing words about one thing, but the music was about something else. It was like having your words say one thing and your heart say something else.

Sometimes it is difficult for us to worship because our minds are filled with many thoughts. The thoughts may not be bad thoughts, but if they keep us from thinking about Jesus, they keep us from worship. They are like a different tune that keeps us from singing what we want to sing.

However, you can still worship Jesus. You can't stop having other thoughts, but you can also think about Jesus. When you think about playing, lunch, or friends, think of Jesus too. Jesus can be with you, no matter what you do. When you remember that he loves you and is always with you, whatever you think about becomes worship.

Example 17
Worship
Related to Sermon on Romans 12:1-8

Two Kinds of Sacrifice

THE WORD
"Make an altar of earth for me, and on it sacrifice your sheep and your cattle as offerings to be completely burned and as fellowship offerings" (Exodus 20:24).

THE WORLD
If at all possible, use this sermon in the front of the church around the altar. You will also need an eight-foot rope—even longer for a larger group of children.

Do you know what we call this piece of furniture *(point to the altar)*? Yes, it is an altar. We use the altar as an important part of our worship. I will read to you from Exod. 20:24, where God tells the Jewish people to build altars. Then we will talk about how we use our altar. *(Read text.)*

They made their altar out of dirt. Then they sacrificed sheep and cattle on the altar. That means they killed the cattle and sheep and burned them. They sacrificed animals for several reasons. One was as a sin offering. They knew they had sinned, and they knew that sin causes death. So they killed the animals to remind themselves of the punishment for sin.

Our altar is made of _____ *(name material)*. We do not use it as a place to sacrifice animals. Instead, we have this cross on it. The cross shows us that Jesus died to pay for our sins. We do not have to bring an animal to die in our place; Jesus has already died for us. But, like the Jewish people, we come to the altar for forgiveness.

The Jewish people used the altar for another reason. They also offered fellowship offerings on the altar. See, when we come close to the altar to receive God's forgiveness, we also come close to one another. Fellowship means to be together. Some Bibles call this a peace offering. We want to be together with other people who also love and worship God.

Let's use this rope as our fellowship offering. *(Lay the rope out full-length in front of the altar.)* Will one of you put the rope on the altar as a sacrifice? Before you do, I should tell you how it must be done: you cannot fold or bend the rope: both ends must be put on the altar at the same time. Now, can you put the rope on the altar as an offering? *(Let several children try, but show that one person cannot do it.)*

You can put the rope on the altar in the way I asked if you work together. *(Have all the children stand on one side of the rope, lift it up, and put it on the altar.)* That was a fellowship offering, because you worked together to do it. No one of you could have done it alone, but you could do it when you helped one another.

We do not give sin offerings at our altar, because Jesus has already paid for our sin. But we can give fellowship offerings. When we come to church, we worship together. We pray not just for ourselves, but also for each other. We sing the songs together. We give our offerings together. We talk to each other and care about each other. We help each other. These acts of worship are our fellowship offerings. Each of us knows we need others, and others need us.

When we worship together, we are living sacrifices as we give ourselves to God and to one another, because Christ gave himself for all of us.

Example 18
Forgiveness
Illustration

Expose Your Sin to the Light

THE WORD

"And when all things are brought out to the light, then their true nature is clearly revealed; for anything that is clearly revealed becomes light" (Ephesians 5:13-14a).

THE WORLD

A cross or crucifix, a camera, and a roll of film that will be wasted. (Reuse the same film if the sermon is used several times. A photographer can give you a film can and some exposed film.)

Listen to what the Bible says, "When all things are brought out to the light, then their true nature is clearly revealed; for anything that is clearly revealed becomes light."

Everything that has happened is going to be made public. All secrets will be gone. All that we have said and done will be known. At first this might scare you. Would you want everyone to know everything you have done and said? None of us would. Let's see how it will work.

Pretend this is a special camera. Most cameras record light on film; that's how we get pictures. Some cameras record heat instead of light; the pictures taken with heat-recording cameras show hot spots and cold spots. But this camera takes pictures of sin.

Remember, we are pretending. When I take a picture of you, it will not show what you look like. Instead, the picture will show your sin. It will show all the bad things that you have said, you have done, and you have thought. Now I'll take a picture of each of you. (*Snap pictures of individuals or groups to include everyone.*)

Remember, the Bible reading said all things must be brought to the light. That means out in the open for everyone to see. But you and I have a special light. Jesus said, "I am the light of the world." He is our light. So let's take the film that shows our sin to him. (*Go to the cross or crucifix. Open the camera and take out the film. Pull the film out of its can and hold it in front of the cross.*)

Do you know what happens to film when it is exposed to light? The pictures on the film disappear. That's why film must always be kept in the dark. This film had a picture of all your sin on it. But when I exposed the film to the light of the cross, all the pictures disappeared. The light removed the pictures. All your sin is gone.

Jesus is the light of the world who takes away our sin because he died to take our punishment. He is the light who takes away darkness. We don't have to hide our sin from him. We don't have to be afraid that he will find out what we have done wrong. Jesus already knows we are sinners. He came to take away our sin and to give us a new life.

Each time you confess your sin, you are taking to Jesus the pictures of what you have done wrong. His light erases the pictures. All your sin is gone. Jesus has taken it away.

Example 19
Creation

I Know Who Will Help

THE WORD
"My help will come from the Lord, who made heaven and earth" (Psalm 121:2).

THE WORLD
A mechanical toy enjoyed by the children present and a sign showing the name of the toy manufacturer. The sign can be a clipping from the toy's box, an ad for the toy, or your own drawing.

Do you recognize this toy? (*Identify it and talk about it. Ask if any children have one like it.*)

Suppose this is your toy. You like it very much. Then it no longer works. You try to fix it, but it still doesn't work. So you take it to your father. He can't fix it either.

But you like this toy, and you know it cost a lot of money. So you take it to a toy shop. The man there tells you that he does not sell this kind of toy. He doesn't know how to fix it. He doesn't know where to send it to be fixed.

You are about to throw the toy away when you see this sign. (*Show sign.*) This is the name of the company that made the toy. You go into a place that has this sign. The person there tells you they can send the toy back to the company that made it. They will fix the toy and give it back to you. They know how to fix it because they made it.

Think about the story of the toy as I read this verse from the Bible: "My help will come from the Lord, who made heaven and earth."

You and I are like the toy in the story that I told. God is like the company that made the toy. When something goes wrong in our lives, we need help. We can look for help in many places. Some people can help us for a little while. But people can also hurt us, even when they want to help us. Friends can help us sometimes, but not all the time. Doctors can help us sometimes, but no one can keep us from dying.

We want to find the one who can *always* help us. Then we see this sign, the one I read from the Bible: "My help will come from the Lord, who made heaven and earth." God knows who we are because he created us. We know who God is because he still claims us.

Our help comes from God. God may help us through others—remember, God also created them. God may help others through us because he also created us.

God loves all people because God created us all. We are not accidents. We were made by God, and God has a reason for us to live. Even though we have not always done what God wants us to do, God still loves us. Instead of being angry at us because of our sin, God sent Jesus to be our Savior and to take away our sin.

When you feel bad about yourself, when things are not going right in your life, remember who created you. Go back to God who loves you and wants to help you. God knows all about you and knows what you need. Let God be the one who helps you.

Example 20
Forgiveness
Small Children

Please Help Myrtle

THE WORD

"Forgive us the wrongs we have done, as we forgive the wrongs that others have done to us" (Matthew 6:12).

THE WORLD

A hand puppet or a small doll. Remove the bottom of a box and hold the puppet in the box so that it cannot be seen.

I brought my friend Myrtle along to church with me today. I wanted you to see her, but she doesn't want to see you. She's in this box, but she won't come out.

Myrtle feels bad about herself. She told a lie this morning. Myrtle knows it is wrong to tell lies. Now she is ashamed of herself and will not come out to talk to you. Do you feel bad when you do something wrong? Then you know how Myrtle feels. She thinks she is no good. She thinks you do not like her because she told a lie.

Do you want to see Myrtle? Do you like her, even if she did do something bad? Of course, you do. But how can you tell Myrtle that you want to be her friend? What can you do to help her come out of the box? (*The children may suggest various things. They may say some of the following or you may make suggestions and respond to them.*)

● "We can say 'Hi' to Myrtle." (*Your reply:*) That's a good idea. Myrtle heard you say "Hi" to her and she liked that.

(Show the head of the puppet outside of the box for a brief moment; then pull it back in.) Myrtle wanted to say "Hi" to you too. But she remembered that she had told a lie and was afraid you wouldn't like her. So she went back in her box.

● "We could give her something to eat." *(Your reply:)* Myrtle would like that. When you give her something you are showing you do like her. *(Again, show the head of the puppet briefly.)* But she still feels bad about herself. Even if you like her, she knows she did something wrong.

● "We can tell her Jesus loves her." *(Your reply:)* That's a good idea. Did you hear that, Myrtle? Jesus loves you. *(Show the head of the doll.)* In fact, Jesus loves you so much that he took away your sins. That's why Jesus died for you. He did it to pay for all the wrong things you have done. He forgives you. *(Have the puppet reach out of the box and wave to the children.)*

See, Myrtle feels good about herself now. She knows that Jesus loves her, and she knows you love her. You helped Myrtle when you showed that you love her and when you told her that Jesus forgave her sins. In the prayer that Jesus taught us, we say, "Forgive us the wrongs we have done, as we forgive the wrongs that others have done to us." You know you are forgiven because Jesus is your Savior. Do you know that you can also give his forgiveness to others?

When other people feel bad about themselves because they have done wrong, you can tell them that Jesus forgives them. You can help them feel good again.

When you feel bad about yourself because you have done wrong things, you can remember that Jesus forgives you. Ask other people to help you remember that Jesus is your Savior. You made Myrtle happy today. You can make other people happy too.

Example 21
Illustration
Forgiving Others

How Can I Forgive Others?

THE WORD
"Then Peter came to Jesus and asked, 'Lord, if my brother keeps on sinning against me, how many times do I have to forgive him? Seven times?'

" 'No, not seven times,' answered Jesus, 'but seventy times seven' " (Matthew 18:21-22).

THE WORLD
A glass pitcher filled with colored water and two glasses—all on a tray.

When Peter asked Jesus how often he had to forgive others, Jesus told this story.

One time a man owed his boss a million dollars. The man could not pay, so the boss was going to throw him into jail. But the man begged for more time. He promised to pay the million dollars back to the boss. The boss felt sorry for the man and forgave him the debt.

Then the man who had been forgiven a million dollar debt found someone else who owed him a few dollars. He asked for the money. The other man couldn't pay and asked for more time. But the first man refused and had the one who owed the few dollars thrown into jail.

When the boss heard this, he was really upset. He called the man back and said, "You worthless slave! I forgave you the whole huge amount you asked me to. You should have had mercy on your fellow servant, just as I had mercy on you." The boss sent the man to jail after all.

Jesus told this story to help us understand how we are to forgive others. Think of this pitcher as Jesus. See the water in it? That is the forgiveness that Jesus earned for us when he died on the cross to pay for our sins. *(Pour water from the pitcher to a glass.)* Jesus gives us forgiveness just as the boss forgave the man his debt of a million dollars.

This glass *(point to the one with water in it)* is you. You have forgiveness, because Christ gave it to you. This glass *(point to empty one)* is someone who has hurt you. You can forgive the other person *(pour water from first glass to the second)* because Christ has forgiven you.

Remember, forgiveness must start with Christ because he is the one who paid for our sins. *(Pour all water back into the pitcher.)* If we start with just two people *(show two empty glasses)*, they cannot forgive one another, because they have no forgiveness to give. But Jesus gives us forgiveness. He always gives us more forgiveness than we need to give others, because he forgives all our sins. When we *have* forgiveness *(pour water into one glass)* we can *give* forgiveness *(pour from first glass into the second)*.

When you think you cannot forgive someone else, it means you have not received the forgiveness you need from Jesus. Go back to Jesus and ask him to forgive all your sins. He will fill you with forgiveness. Then you will have forgiveness to give to others.

You can't give away something that you don't have. If you cannot forgive others, it means you have run out of forgiveness. That is the time to remember where forgiveness comes from. Go back to Jesus, and he will fill you with love and forgiveness. Then you can give it to others.

Example 22
Use of the Law

In the Name of Christ
We Command

THE WORD

"In the name of the Lord Jesus Christ we command these people and warn them to lead orderly lives and work to earn their own living" (2 Thessalonians 3:12).

THE WORLD

A credit card.

I want you to listen to part of a verse from the Bible. It says, "We command these people and warn them to lead orderly lives and work to earn their own living." That means the people are to get to work and do what's right.

The Bible has many commands. Listen to some of them. Don't tell lies. Use God's name in the right way. Love all people. Don't steal. Don't call people bad names. All these commands tell you what you should do—and what you should not do. And they scare us because we don't always do what they tell us to do.

To understand the commands in the Bible, let's take a more simple command. This one is not from the Bible, but from me: go to (*name a local store*) and buy a TV set for me. Can you do that? The TV set might cost $500. If you do what I told you to do, you will have to pay for it. Do you have $500 with you?

Now let me change the command just a little: here is my credit card; go to *(the store)* and buy a TV set for me. Now you can do it, because you can charge it to my account. If the store manager phones me and asks if you can charge it to my account, I will say yes. You can do what I asked you to do because I gave you a way to do it.

Before, I told you I was reading only a part of a verse to you; now I will read the entire verse. It says, "In the name of the Lord Jesus Christ we command these people and warn them to lead orderly lives and work to earn their own living."

When I read it the first time, I told you to get to work and do what was right. But this time it was different. This time it said, "In the name of Christ get to work and do what is right." When you hear any command in the name of Christ, it is a new command. Christ lived a perfect life. Then he died to pay for our sins. He took our sin and gave us his goodness. Now he helps us do good.

When I command you to do something in the name of Christ, it is like giving you his credit card. Just as I could let you charge the TV set to my account, Jesus lets you charge your sins to his account. So your sins are forgiven.

But he does even more than that. He also lets us use his credit to do good. We can't do all the things the Bible tells us to do if we depend on ourselves. When we are told to do something in the name of Christ, we can do it with Christ's power. He helps us.

When you hear a command from the Bible, listen carefully. Because Jesus is your Savior, he will help you do what the command tells you to do. Always hear each command in the name of Jesus.

Example 23
Definition of Grace and Faith

Saved by Grace through Faith

THE WORD
"For it is by God's grace that you have been saved through faith" (Ephesians 2:8).

THE WORLD
A chalkboard or large piece of paper with GOD written at the top and YOU at the bottom and a piece of chalk or a marker pencil.

The Bible says, "For it is by God's grace that you have been saved through faith." That makes grace and faith very important. You are saved by grace through faith. That means you will go to heaven by grace through faith. That means God saves you from problems here on earth by grace through faith.

Do you know what grace is? How does God save you through grace? Do you know what faith is? How are you saved through faith? Those are important words. So let's talk about them.

Grace belongs to God. It is God's grace, but he gives it to us. So grace goes this way: *(Draw a line from GOD to YOU and put an arrowhead at the bottom showing its direction to YOU. Write GRACE beside the line.)* God gave his grace to you when he sent Jesus to be your Savior. Jesus gives you forgiveness of sins and eternal life. Those are gifts of God's grace to you. You are saved by grace.

Now let's look at faith. We believe in God. Therefore faith starts down here *(point to YOU)*. You trust in God. You have faith in him. Therefore your faith reaches to God. *(Draw a line from YOU to GOD. Put an arrowhead at the top to show its direction. Write FAITH by the line.)*

God gives you the gift of salvation. That's grace—see, it is from God to you. Faith receives that gift. You trust in God because Jesus has died for you. You believe he rose from the dead to give you eternal life. That's faith.

Your faith does not earn salvation. It is a gift. Your faith trusts in the gift that God has given.

Grace must always come first. Grace gives you something to believe. If your faith is weak, you cannot make it strong. Instead, God makes it strong by giving more grace. *(Connect the lines at the bottom near the word YOU.)* God's grace comes through you to give you faith.

If you want others to believe in Jesus, you cannot give them faith, but you can offer them grace. You can tell them what Jesus has done for them. The grace that God gives to them in Jesus will give them something to believe. Then they too can have faith.

Example 24
Definition of Church

What Is the Church?

THE WORD

"[Christ] did this to dedicate the church to God by his word, after making it clean by washing it in water, in order to present the church to himself in all its beauty—pure and faultless, without spot or wrinkle or any other imperfection" (Ephesians 5:26-27).

THE WORLD

The building where the children worship.

Can you show me a church? Is this building the church? Let's listen to how the Bible describes the church. It says, "[Christ] did this [that is, he gave his life] to dedicate the church to God by his word, after making it clean by washing it in water, in order to present the church to himself in all its beauty— pure and faultless, without spot or wrinkle or any other imperfection."

If the church is a building, the Bible says Jesus died in order that we could have a beautiful and perfect building. Jesus did not love a building; he loved people. He died for us to take away our sins, so that we can be holy and perfect in his sight.

Yet we say this is the church. And in one way we are right. Let's look for the church right here. If we got rid of all the pews, would this still be the church? Could we get rid of the organ? the windows? the door? the carpets? What else could we get rid of and still be the church? What if the roof were gone? Would we still be a church? What if the pulpit were gone? the cross? the hymnals?

We've talked about what we could get rid of and still be a church. What would we have to keep to still be the church? Look around and see what we would need. Yes, we would need the Word of God—though we wouldn't need all of these Bibles. We would need Baptism—though we wouldn't need that baptismal font. We would need the Lord's Supper—though we would not need the fancy dishes for it that we have here.

But we would need all those things for a special reason. The church is people—people who believe Jesus is their Savior. We could get rid of all the other things and still be the church. Jesus loves people. He died for people. He has made us clean by washing us in our baptism. He makes us pure and faultless because he takes away our sin.

When you come to church, you are not coming to the building. Instead, you are coming to be with the people, the people who also believe that Jesus is their Savior. Other people come here to be with you; you are also a part of the church because Jesus is your Savior.

Example 25
Definition of Grace

Are You Sure You Are Saved?

THE WORD
"But by the free gift of God's grace all are put right with him through Christ Jesus, who sets them free" (Romans 3:24).

THE WORLD
A chalkboard, chalk, and eraser.

Are you sure you are saved? Do you know that God is with you now and that he loves you? Do you know you will go to heaven? I hope you are sure that you will be saved. I also hope you are sure for the right reason.

The Bible tells you that you can be sure. It says, "But by the free gift of God's grace all are put right with him through Christ Jesus, who sets them free."

Let's look at it this way. Here is a problem: *(Put the following on the chalkboard.)*

What I do:	_____ %	
What Jesus did:	+	_____ %
	100%	

For you to be 100% sure that you are saved, you must add what part you have done and what part Jesus has done to make a total of 100%.

Suppose we divide it 50/50. *(Write in 50% on each line.)* That means Jesus has earned half of your salvation; you, the other half. You can be sure of the part that Jesus did, but could you be sure of the part you did?

We had better change that to 90/10. *(Change the figures.)* That means Jesus earned 90% of your salvation; you, the other 10%. You can be sure of the part that Jesus did, but can you be sure of your part?

We had better change that to 99/1. *(Change the figures.)* That means Jesus has paid for 99% of your salvation, and you have done 1%. Again, you can be sure of Jesus doing his part, but what about your part? Do you want to trust in yourself even for 1% of your salvation?

By now you see there is only one way that you can be sure that you are saved: Jesus earned 100% of your salvation, and you 0%. *(Change the figures.)* The only way you can be sure that you are saved is to trust totally in Jesus—and not at all in yourself.

Remember the Bible verse I read. It says that you are put right with God by a free gift of God's grace. God gave you his grace through Jesus Christ, who died for you. Jesus has set you free from sin. You don't have to worry. You are saved. Jesus did it all. You can depend on him.

Example 26
Baptism
Sense of Touch

When Jesus Washes Us

THE WORD
"Christ loved the church and gave his life for it. He did this to dedicate the church to God by his word, after making it clean by washing it in water" (Ephesians 5:25b-26).

THE WORLD
A bowl of clean, warm water and a dish of mud.

When someone is baptized, something happens. We are doing something in the name of Jesus Christ and by the power of God's Word. Let me show you what happens in Baptism.

See this hand *(show one hand)*; it is nice and clean. But look what happens to my other hand. *(Put your other hand in the mud and show the dirty hand.)* Now I have one clean hand and one dirty hand. But don't worry! I also have a separate bowl of water here to wash my dirty hand.

Watch what happens to my hands. You do it this way all the time. I use the clean hand to wash the dirty hand. As I use the clean hand to rub the dirt off the dirty one *(illustrate)*, the clean hand gets dirty. For a short time they are both dirty. Now both are clean. *(Show both hands.)*

The way I washed my hands will help us understand what happens when someone is baptized. Listen to what Paul says in Ephesians: "Christ loved the church and gave his life for it. He did this to dedicate the church to God by his word, after making it clean by washing it in water."

Christ is like the clean hand. He is the holy Son of God. Each of us is like the dirty hand. We have the dirt of sin that brings death to all people. But Christ gave his life for us—as he did for all people. He became the clean hand that washed the dirty one. Our dirt, our sin, stuck to him. Our sin killed him. But his death washed us clean—just as one hand washes another. One Savior of the world has washed away the sins of all people.

This washing has happened to each of us. It happens when Christ by his Word makes us clean as he washes us in the water, and we then become a part of the church that he dedicates to God.

Example 27
Christmas

The Star Above and the One Below

THE WORD

"And so they [the visitors from the East] left, and on their way they saw the same star they had seen in the East. When they saw it, how happy they were, what joy was theirs! It went ahead of them until it stopped over the place where the child was" (Matthew 2:9-10).

THE WORLD

A book that uses an asterisk and a footnote, a Christmas tree with a star on top, and a creche with a baby under it.

I want to see if you know something special about reading a book. If you are reading and see a star like this, which is called an asterisk *(point to it)*, do you know what it means? Let me show you. The star up here means there will be another star down here at the bottom of the page. *(Show star on page.)* The star at the bottom of the page explains something about what is said by the star at the top of the page.

Now let me show you something about another star. See that star at the top of the Christmas tree? That star is like an asterisk. It tells us to look down below. See what is here. *(Show the baby in the creche.)* This is a figure of a little baby that tells us Jesus was born. God became a human being and was born on this earth to be with us.

Some Wise Men from the East who studied the stars in the skies were the first to see the special star when Jesus was born. They followed the star for many miles. Then the Bible tells us, "On their way they saw the same star they had seen in the East. When they saw it, how happy they were, what joy was theirs! It went ahead of them until it stopped over the place where the child was."

The Wise Men first saw the star in the sky; then they looked down and saw where the baby Jesus was. The star above led them to see the Savior below. They were happy to see the star—not just because they liked stars or because the star was pretty. They were happy to see the star because it showed the way for them to find the baby Jesus.

We use lots of stars in our Christmas decorations. When you see a star on trees, on cards, or in windows, let each star remind you to look down. God is not far away up in the sky. God has come down to earth to be with us. Jesus is God who lived with us. He died to pay for our sins. He lives again as the Lord in heaven, but also as the Savior who is with us.

Every Christmas star is a reminder. Each one tells you to look down to see the Savior who is with you. When you read books that have the little stars called asterisks, remember the Christmas star. Each star tells you that you will see even more when you look down for another star. When you see Jesus, you learn more about God's love and grace for you.

Example 28
Epiphany

You Can Be a Star

THE WORD

"Do everything without complaining or arguing, so that you may be innocent and pure as God's perfect children, who live in a world of corrupt and sinful people. You must shine among them like stars lighting up the sky, as you offer them the message of life" (Philippians 2:14-16a).

THE WORLD

If possible, use an available light in the room that can be seen as it is reflected by a window. If necessary, place a light where it cannot be seen except as a reflection in a mirror or window. Turn off all lights in the room and close the blinds to make the room as dark as possible.

I have turned off all the lights to remind you of something from our Bible reading. It says we live in a world of corrupt and sinful people. The room is dark to remind us that sin hides the beauty of God's world. Sin keeps us from seeing all the good things God wants us to have. Our Bible reading also says that we add to the darkness of sin when we argue and complain. When we argue and complain, we keep ourselves and others from seeing the blessings of God.

But we don't have to add to the problem of sin. Our Bible reading also says we can shine in the world of sin like a star that lights up the sky. I'm going to ask you all to look this way (*point toward the window or mirror*). Tell me when you see a light. *(Turn on the light.)* There, do you see the light? *(Direct everyone's attention to the reflection.)* We now have a light.

Do you really see the light? What do you see? You see the reflection of the light. Where is the real light? *(Help them find the light.)* Because the light is here, we can see the reflection over there. This *(point to the light)* is the source of light. This *(point to mirror or window)* is a reflection of the light.

When our Bible reading tells us we can be stars to give light in the world of sin, it does not mean we can be like this light. We can't make the light. Jesus is the light of the world. He is God who became a person and lived with us. He took away the darkness of sin when he died for us. He gave us light when he rose from the dead. When we hear what Jesus has done for us, his light shines on us.

We are like the reflected light. When Jesus' light shines on us, it bounces back so others can see it. Some people have not seen Jesus. But when they see what Jesus has done to us, we become like stars that give light to them. Because Jesus is with us, we don't have to argue and complain. He helps us. His light shows us all God's blessings.

Our Bible reading says that when we tell people the message of life, we are stars that light the world of darkness. When we tell others about Jesus, we are giving them the message of life.

You can be a star. You are a star when you see what Jesus has done for you, and when you share that love with others.

Example 29
Lent

Hit Me Instead

THE WORD
"But because of our sins he was wounded, beaten because of the evil we did. We are healed by the punishment he suffered, made whole by the blows he received" (Isaiah 53:5).

THE WORLD
Two children.

Adam and Brian *(call two children by name)*, will you come up here to help me? I know you are friends, but I'm going to ask you to pretend you are angry at each other. I know that all of us get angry sometimes. Often our anger causes problems. We do and say things that make the problems even worse. I'm asking you to pretend you are angry so that we can learn a better way to get rid of our anger.

Adam, if you were mad at Brian, what would you do? Don't do it yet—just show us! How would your face look if you were angry? How would your hand look?

Brian, if you saw Adam looking like that, how would you feel? Would you get angry too? Would your hand and face look the same way?

I want the rest of you to see what two angry people look like. That's probably how you look when you are angry. When people are angry, they generally do something that causes big problems. Families have fights; friends get mad and won't talk to each other anymore; nations go to war with one another.

But the Bible tells us there is another way to get rid of our anger. Listen to what an Old Testament prophet named Isaiah wrote. He told us about the Savior who was coming to save us from our sins. This is what he said the Savior would do: "But because of our sins he was wounded, beaten because of the evil we did. We are healed by the punishment he suffered, made whole by the blows he received."

Isaiah said that the Savior would take the pain we should receive. Let's see how that works. Adam and Brian, pretend you are angry again, and pretend I am Jesus. Adam, you are ready to hit Brian, but hit me instead. It is Brian who did the wrong that makes you angry, and you want to hit him to pay him back. But you can hit me instead. I'll take the punishment instead.

You don't want to hit me, because you're not angry at me. But I don't want you to hit Brian, because I love him and I don't want him to be hurt. And I love you too, so I don't want Brian to hurt you either. He also can hit me instead.

When Jesus died on the cross, he let all the people of the world hit him. He took the punishment for our sins. He said we don't have to hurt each other any more. He loves us all, and he doesn't want us to hurt one another.

When you are angry at someone else, remember that Jesus died to forgive that person. You don't have to hurt that person. Jesus has taken the wrong away.

When someone else is angry at you, you don't have to let the person hurt you. Jesus loves you. Ask for forgiveness instead of punishment.

Always see Jesus standing between you and the other person. (*Stand between the two children.*) When Jesus puts his love between you and another person, you can love one another. All the anger is gone. Jesus took it away.

Example 30
Palm Sunday

Perfect Praise

THE WORD
"The chief priests and the teachers of the Law became angry when they saw the wonderful things [Jesus] was doing and the children shouting in the Temple, 'Praise to David's Son!' So they asked Jesus, 'Do you hear what they are saying?'

" 'Indeed I do,' answered Jesus. 'Haven't you read this scripture? "You have trained children and babies to offer perfect praise" ' " (Matthew 21:15-16).

THE WORLD
A picture (on an Easter theme) drawn by a child.

Look at this picture. *(Describe it briefly.)* Suppose this picture is on the church bulletin board. Two women look at it. Woman A says, "Look at the mistakes on that picture. The colors do not go together. It is not neat." Woman B looks at the picture and says, "That's a beautiful picture. It is perfect."

Which of the two women is the mother of the child who drew the picture? How do you know? The mother liked the picture because she loves the child who drew it. Because of her love, she saw good things in the picture. Woman A did not like the picture because she did not know the person who drew it.

I told you the story about the picture and the two women to help you understand something from the Bible. Let me read it to you, "The chief priests and the teachers of the Law became angry when they saw the wonderful things [Jesus] was doing and the children shouting in the Temple, "Praise to David's Son!" So they asked Jesus, "Do you hear what they are saying?" "Indeed I do," answered Jesus. "Haven't you read this scripture? 'You have trained children and babies to offer perfect praise.' "

The children in this story were happy. When they saw Jesus, they sang, "Praise to David's Son!" David had been the king of Israel. These children knew that Jesus was a king too. They treated him like a king.

Some of the adults did not like that. The chief priests and the teachers of the law were like Woman A. They found fault with what the children did. They complained about the song.

But another adult liked what the children did. Jesus was like Woman B. He quoted a psalm that says children and babies can offer perfect praise. Jesus thought the children's song was beautiful. Maybe all the children could not sing perfectly. Maybe they didn't all sing the same notes and words, as a choir would. But the song was perfect to Jesus because he loved them. Just as Woman B thought this picture was perfect because her child drew it, Jesus thought the children's praise was perfect because he loved those children.

Jesus loves your praise too. You can say what those children said. Let's all say, "Praise to David's Son." We praise Jesus because he is our Savior. He is the one who died as the sacrifice to pay for our sins. He is the one who rose from the dead to give us eternal life. He is the perfect Savior, so we can praise him.

You praise Jesus when you sing songs about him, when you worship him. You praise him when you serve him by helping others. When Jesus sees and hears your praise, he thinks it is perfect. It is perfect because he makes it perfect for us.

Example 31
Baptism at Easter

It's a Date!

THE WORD

"For surely you know that when we were baptized into union with Christ Jesus, we were baptized into union with his death. By our baptism, then, we were buried with him and shared his death, in order that, just as Christ was raised from death by the glorious power of the Father, so also we might live a new life" (Romans 6:3-4).

THE WORLD

Three appointment books—including one for the current year.

Today Rose is being baptized. This Baptism is in my appointment book. See, I have it here. (*Show date, time of the Baptism, and the person's name.*)

This Baptism is also recorded in another book. In Rom. 6:3 we read, "For surely you know that when we were baptized into union with Christ Jesus, we were baptized into union with his death."

When Rose is baptized, she is baptized into union with Christ. When we scheduled this Baptism in this appointment book, we made a date with Jesus. Rose is being baptized in his name. She will be in union with him.

But this is not the first date that Jesus made with Rose. A long time ago Jesus had another appointment with Rose. Pretend this appointment book was for the year that Jesus died.

They didn't have appointment books then, but Jesus did pick a time and place to die for the sins of the world. He made a date to die for Rose. When she is baptized today, she is baptized into union with his death from long ago.

Jesus made a date to die for Rose long ago *(hold up first book)*. He has a date to be with her as she is baptized today *(hold up second book)*. And he has still another date for her. The next verse of Romans 6 says, "By our baptism, then, we were buried with him and shared his death, in order that, just as Christ was raised from death by the glorious power of the Father, so also we might live a new life."

Jesus gives Rose a new life. Because he arose from the dead and destroyed the power of sin and death, she can have a new life. He makes another appointment with her. *(Show third book.)* Sometime in the far future, he has another date with her. Just as he rose from the dead, he will also raise her from the dead.

As all of us take part in this Baptism today, we see that Rose is baptized into union with Christ. His death and his resurrection from the dead become a part of her life.

Example 32
Small children
Valentine's Day

Love God with All Your Heart

THE WORD

"Love the Lord your God with all your heart, with all your soul, and with all your strength" (Deuteronomy 6:5).

THE WORLD

Prior to starting the worship service, pin a large red heart over your own heart. Also put a small red heart in your shoe, another in your wallet or purse. Put a heart in your hair, and stick another one on your hand.

Can you see my heart? No, my real heart is in my chest. But look at this heart on my chest. This is the kind of heart we use on Valentine's Day to show we love someone. I want you to see the heart on my chest. That reminds me that I love Jesus. The Bible says, "Love the Lord your God with all your heart." Because Jesus loves us, we can love him. Jesus loved us with all of his heart when he died on the cross to pay for our sins. He gave his life for us. Now we love him with all of our hearts. The heart has become a sign of love. That's why we use hearts on Valentine's Day. We want to show our love for each other.

The Bible also says something else. It says, "Love the Lord your God with all your heart, with all your soul, and with all your strength." You can love God with your heart, but you can love him in other ways too.

111

Look at this *(show the heart on your hand)*. I can love Jesus with my strength. I can love him by what I do with my hands. When I use my hand to help someone, I am showing my love for Jesus. Look at this *(show the heart in your shoe)*. I can love Jesus when I walk. See this *(show the heart in your hair)*. I can love Jesus by the way I think. Or look at this *(show the heart in your wallet or purse)*. I can love Jesus by the way I spend my money.

We love God with our hearts, but we can love him in many other ways too. Can you think of other ways that we can love God? *(Place the heart on your mouth.)* Can we love God by the way we speak? *(Place the heart on your ears.)* Can we love God by the way we listen to him and others? *(Let the children think of other places they could put the heart to show ways they can love God. Suggestions: on their toys, on their school desk, their lunch box, etc.)*

We can love God with all parts of our lives. When Jesus gave himself to us, he gave all of his life. He even died for us so we can live forever with him. He gave us not only his heart, but he gave all of his life. We can also love him with all of our lives.

Example 33
Mother's or Father's Day

See What Your Parents Have to Give

THE WORD

"Children, it is your Christian duty to obey your parents, for this is the right thing to do. 'Respect your father and mother' is the first commandment that has a promise added: 'so that all may go well with you, and you may live a long time in the land.' " (Ephesians 6:1-3).

THE WORLD

A family heirloom—a piece of jewelry, dish, or something that may be passed from one generation to the next.

Today we give special honor to parents. Listen to a reading from the Bible that gives you two reasons for you to obey your parents. It says, "Children, it is your Christian duty to obey your parents, for this is the right thing to do. 'Respect your father and mother' is the first commandment that has a promise added: 'so that all may go well with you, and you may live a long time in the land.' "

First, you obey your parents because it is the right thing to do. Second, God gives a special promise to those who respect their parents. He says all will go well with them, and they will live a long time in the land.

This promise does not mean that people who respect their parents will live longer than those who don't. Remember, this comes from the Commandments that were given to the Jewish people when they were on the way to the promised land. God promised the people that if parents taught their children and children learned from their parents, their nation would last a long time.

This promise applies to us in a different way. Parents have something to give to children. Children need something from parents. If both parents and children do as God planned, all will go well with them, and their family, their nation, and their church will last a long time.

Let me show you how this works. This is a family treasure. (*Show and explain the heirloom.*) A long time ago parents gave it to their child. That child became a parent who gave it to the next generation. But suppose there was a child who showed no respect for his parents, one who would not listen to them or obey them, one who would not accept their love, one who did not want to be a part of their family. How could the parents give him the family treasure? He would not appreciate it because he does not respect the family; he would throw it away or sell it. So he would not receive the treasure.

Maybe your family does have a treasure that will be yours when you grow up. It might be something like this, or a book, or a picture.

There is one treasure that each family has. It has been passed from parents to children for many years. That treasure is the gospel of Christ.

You parents have this treasure because others have given it to you. They have told you that Jesus is your Savior. They have shown you his love and forgiveness. Now you offer that treasure to your children. You have done that by bringing them to church today. You do it in your home.

Children, listen to your parents. Obey them and respect them. Then you will receive the treasure of Jesus' love, and you can pass it on to your children.

Example 34
National Holiday

God Asked Someone to Help You

THE WORD

"For the sake of the Lord submit yourselves to every human authority: to the Emperor, who is the supreme authority, and to the governors, who have been appointed by him to punish the evildoers and to praise those who do good" (1 Peter 2:13-14).

THE WORLD

If possible, a pet hamster, guinea pig, or white mouse. If not, a toy mouse will do. In either case, it should be in a cage.

Brad was excited. He had a new pet. See it. *(If you use a toy, ask the children to pretend it is real.)* Brad's mother said the family needed some rules about taking care of the new pet. Since they also had a dog, the hamster had to stay in the cage when the dog was in the house. Whoever let the hamster out of the cage had to watch where it went. They also had to clean the cage and see that the pet had food and water.

Brad was glad to follow the rules that his mother made. He knew they were good rules that would protect his hamster. If everyone followed the rules, the family, the dog, and the hamster could all live together and enjoy each other.

Today we are celebrating an important holiday for our country. We want to thank God for the blessings he has given us in our country. We also want to learn how to use the blessings God has given us. Listen to what the Bible says to us about our government, "For the sake of the Lord submit yourselves to every human authority: to the Emperor, who is the supreme authority, and to the governors, who have been appointed by him to punish the evildoers and to praise those who do good."

Brad's family had to have rules to help them take good care of their pets. We also need rules for us to live together in our country. God has also given us leaders to help us.

First, God gives us rulers who help us by punishing those who do evil. Our government makes rules to protect our lives and property. We have rules about driving safely on the roads for the good of everyone. We have rules that protect us from bad food and other harmful things.

Our government also helps us receive good things. It provides education and recreation. The government helps us have good medicine and retirement.

The Bible tells us to obey our government for the sake of the Lord. God sends us his blessings in many ways. He sent Jesus to be our Savior. Jesus makes us a part of God's kingdom now, so we can live with God. Jesus will take us to heaven. But God also gives us government here on earth so we can live together at peace.

Think of all the people who work for the government to help us. Can you name some? (*Answers might include police, armed forces, teachers, local officials, court employees. You might ask adults present who work for the government to stand.*) Each of these people are sent by God to punish those who do evil and reward those who do good.

Example 35
Sunday School Rally Day

Find a Good Example

THE WORD
"Now, all of this is an example for us, to warn us not to desire evil things, as they did, nor to worship idols, as some of them did" (1 Corinthians 10:6-7a).

THE WORLD
Yourself and the children.

I am going to show you two ways that I could greet you when you come for the children's sermon. You decide which way you like best.

First, I can be friendly: "Good morning, boys and girls. I am glad to see you here." *(Shake hands with or touch several of the children. Give some "good strokes" by commenting on their appearance.)* That's one example.

Here is another example: "Stop making so much noise! Sit down and be quiet! If you are going to be in church, you should learn how to behave. I'm going to tell your parents that you weren't good in church today."

Which of the two examples did you like best? When I was friendly, was it easy for you to be friendly too? When I was rude, did you feel like being rude too?

We all learn from one another. We follow each other's examples. Sometimes we follow good examples, sometimes we follow bad examples. The Bible tells us something about following examples. First, it tells some of the Old Testament stories about people. Then it says, "Now, all of this is an example for us, to warn us not to desire evil things, as they did, nor to worship idols as some of them did."

The Bible tells us many stories so that we can learn from the example of others. Many of the examples are good examples. From the Bible we learn about people like David, Ruth, Paul, Esther, and many others. They were people who trusted God and served him. We would like to follow their example.

The Bible also tells us about bad examples. Judas and Saul are bad examples. We would not want to follow their example.

The people in the Bible who are good examples were not perfect people. All the heroes and heroines of the Bible also did wrong things. But when they did wrong, they admitted they were wrong, and they asked God to forgive them. The Old Testament people knew God would send a Savior. The New Testament people knew Jesus. They knew he died to take away their sin. They were good examples, not because they sinned, but because they admitted their sin and asked for God's forgiveness through Jesus.

We teach Bible stories in Sunday school so that you can learn about the people who are examples for us. We want you to know about the people in the Bible because they are examples of how God works in the lives of people. The Bible stories show how God lives with people and how people can live with God. When you know the Bible stories, you will know what God does and says in the lives of people.

Today you go into a new Sunday school class. There you can learn more about the examples of people in the Bible. You can also be an example to others who see you go to Sunday school. Maybe they will follow your example and go to Sunday school with you.

Example 36
First Day of School

A Way to Start

THE WORD

"Reverence for the Lord is an education in itself. You must be humble before you can ever receive honors" (Proverbs 15:33).

THE WORLD

A school bag filled with the things a student needs as school starts: books, tablet, pencil, ruler, crayons, etc. (include things for each grade level of children present).

Are you ready for school to start? What do you already have? What do you still need? Here are some things you will need for school this year. *(Briefly show the items and discuss why each is needed.)*

I'm going to read something from the Bible that tells you what else you need for school this year. This is from Prov. 15:33. It says, "Reverence for the Lord is an education in itself. You must be humble before you can ever receive honors."

To get an education, you need reverence for the Lord. Reverence is a big word, so let's talk about it. If you have reverence for someone, you respect that person, you are in awe of him, you are impressed by the person, and you appreciate him. If you have reverence for someone, you know how great that person is—especially as compared to yourself.

To get an education, you need reverence for the Lord. In science classes you will learn about plants, animals, and minerals. Your reverence for the Lord will help you understand and enjoy all the wonderful things of science.

In other classes you will learn about people. You will study those who have lived before us in history. You will see the pictures they drew and read the books they wrote. You will learn what makes people happy and what makes them sad. Your reverence for the Lord will help you understand people. You will see how God loves people. You will know that Jesus loves all people. When you have reverence for the Lord, you can know more about people. You know they have all done wrong things, and you know they are forgiven and they can do many good things.

When you have reverence for the Lord, you recognize how great God is and how much you need him. Then you know that you don't know everything, that you have a lot to learn. That Bible verse also says, "You must be humble before you can ever receive honors." You must be humble enough to listen to others if you are to learn from them. If you want to graduate with honors (that means you do real well) you must start with humility (that means, you know you have a lot to learn.)

This bag has a lot of things in it that you will need in school. Remember, you also need reverence for the Lord. I can't show you reverence to put in this bag with the other things you need in school. But I can show you my reverence for the Lord because I love Jesus, I worship him, and I serve him. I see your reverence for the Lord because you are here today to worship Jesus too. You also love him. You also serve him. Remember that when you are in school, and you'll have a great year!

Example 37
Small Children
Reformation

You Will Be Free

THE WORD

"So Jesus said to those who believed in him, 'If you obey my teaching, you are really my disciples; you will know the truth, and the truth will set you free' " (John 8:31).

THE WORLD

A toy dog and a rope about four feet long.

I want you to meet one of my friends. *(Show toy.)* This is Fido. I'll tell you a story about Fido.

The family who owned Fido first lived in an apartment. Then they moved to a house with a big yard. They thought the yard would be good for Fido. He had always stayed inside before; now he could go outside.

However, the family's new home was on a busy street with lots of cars. They were afraid that Fido would get out, run in the street, and be hit by a car. So every time someone took Fido outside, they put this rope around his neck. *(Tie rope around toy dog.)* When Fido started to run, they could pull him back and keep him away from the traffic. If they left Fido outside, they tied the rope to a tree. He could still run and play—but only this far *(show the length of the rope).*

After a while Fido learned to stay in the backyard. He came to know that it belonged to him and his family. So they took the rope off. Because Fido had learned to stay in the yard, he could be free from the rope.

I told you the story about Fido to help you understand something from the Bible. Jesus said, "If you obey my teaching, you are really my disciples; you will know the truth, and the truth will set you free."

God is like the family that owned Fido. He wants us to be free and to enjoy the whole world. But we sometimes use our freedom in the wrong way and get hurt. Fido would have been hurt if he had been allowed on the street. We hurt ourselves and others when we sin. The family put Fido on a rope to protect him. God gave us rules to protect us. God has told us what to do and what not to do.

The rules that God gives us are like this rope. They tell us we can go only so far—and no farther. God gave us the rules to protect us. But he still wants us to be free. So God sent Jesus to be our Savior. Jesus died for us to pay for our sins. He also lives again to help us fight against sin. When we know the truth about Jesus, we are free. Jesus has set us free.

Remember that Fido was free from the rope when he learned to stay in the yard. We are free when we learn that Jesus forgives us and helps us fight against sin. We are free from the law. That does not mean we are free *to sin*; it means we are free *from sin*. Jesus has paid the price of sin. He frees us from the need to sin.

When we are with Jesus, we are free. We are free to enjoy the wonderful world God made for us. We are free, because we know the truth about Jesus.

Example 38
Reformation

Here I Stand

THE WORD

"I have complete confidence in the gospel; it is God's power to save all who believe, first the Jews and also the Gentiles. For the gospel reveals how God puts people right with himself: it is through faith from beginning to end" (Romans 1:16-17).

THE WORLD

The following symbols on large sheets of paper: a cross, a dollar sign, the letter A, and a ticket. Tape the papers at various places in the front of the worship area.

Do you know what it means to stand in line? You may have to stand in line to get a drink or to catch a bus. You may have to stand in line when you buy something. When you stand in line, you want to make sure it is the right line.

I have four places in the front of the church for you to stand in line. Can you see the four places? *(Show them.)* Andy *(call a child by name),* which line would you stand in if you wanted money? *(Have him stand by the dollar sign.)* Miriam *(call another child),* which line would you stand in if you wanted to get the best report card? *(Have her stand by the A.)* Nicol *(call a third child),* which line would you stand in if you wanted to go to a concert? *(Have her stand by the ticket.)* Brian *(call a fourth child),* which line would you stand in if you wanted to go to heaven? *(If he chooses the cross immediately, ask him why. If he does not, ask others to help him decide. In a discussion include the following ideas: the cross is a sign that tells us Jesus died for us when he paid for our sins and that he rose again to give us a new life; we can go to heaven because Jesus is our Savior.)*

It was easy for Brian to find the right line to stand in when he wants to go to heaven. He knew about Jesus because we talk about the gospel often. The gospel is the good news that Jesus is our Savior.

But it was not always that way. A long time ago some people thought they had to buy their way to heaven. They would have stood in the line with the dollar sign. Some thought they had to know the right answers to go to heaven. They would have stood by the A. Some thought they had to get a ticket to go to heaven by doing good works. They looked for the ticket line.

At that time a man named Martin Luther studied the Bible. He read this verse. "I have complete confidence in the gospel; it is God's power to save all who believe, first the Jews and also the Gentiles. For the gospel reveals how God puts people right with himself; it is through faith from beginning to end."

When Luther read that, he moved to a different line. He stood here *(point to the cross)*. Many people became angry at him. Some wanted to kill him if he did not stop telling others that they were saved by faith in Jesus without trying to earn their own salvation. But Luther would not move back to the other lines. He said, "Here I stand. I cannot do otherwise." Luther stood by the gospel as the only way to live here on earth and the only way to go to heaven.

When we celebrate the Reformation today, we go to this line *(point to the cross)* and stand here. We stand by the gospel because we know it is God's power to save all who believe. When we see what Jesus has done for us, we believe him and receive his power.

Example 39
Thanksgiving

Thanks for the Past and the Future

THE WORD:
"Every day I will thank you [God];
I will praise you forever and ever. . . .
What you have done will be praised
from one generation to the next;
they will proclaim your mighty acts" (Psalm 145:2, 4).

THE WORLD
A cornucopia filled with symbols of blessings.

Today we thank God for all the blessings he gives us. Even though today is Thanksgiving Day, it is not the only time when we should thank God. Listen to what Psalm 145 tells us. (*Read text.*) The psalm writer says that he thanks God today, that he will thank God in the future, and that each generation will remember God's blessings from the past.

Let's do something to help understand how each generation thanks God. Will you all stand up in a row? (*Help the children stand in a line, all facing the same direction, and about two feet apart.*) Nathan (*a child in the middle of the line*) will represent this generation. The one behind him stands for your parents; the next one, your grandparents; the next, your great-grand-parents; and so on, back into history. These are the past generations. The person in front of Nathan stands for your children, the next one is your grandchildren, and so on. These are the future generations.

Today we thank God. (*Give Nathan the cornucopia.*) With the psalm we say, "Every day I will praise you." But all of today's blessings came from the past. The food we eat came from seeds and animals that lived long ago. (*Pass the cornucopia to the children behind Nathan.*) Today we thank God for our country. People for many generations have made it possible for us to have freedom. Today we thank God that Jesus is our Savior. The good news that Jesus died to pay for our sins and rose to give us eternal life has been passed from generation to generation since the time Jesus lived on earth. As we thank God today, we also do what the psalmist said, "What you have done will be praised from one generation to the next; they will proclaim your mighty acts." As we thank God for what we have today, we also remember what he has done in the past. We thank him for that too.

Today we also remember the future. The psalm says, "I will praise you forever and ever." (*Give the cornucopia back to Nathan.*) The blessings we have today will also be passed on to the future. (*Pass the cornucopia to the children ahead of Nathan.*) As we thank God for the blessings we have today, we also think about those who will live after us.

When we thank God for food, we remember it came from him and that we are to take good care of the earth so that those who live after us will also have food. When we thank God for our country, we also remember that we are to work to keep freedom so that those who follow us will have freedom too. When we thank God that Jesus is our Savior, we remember that we are to tell others so that those who live after us will also know about Jesus. Thank you, God, for the past, for now, and for the future. Amen.

Example 40
Installation of Pastor or Teacher

Someone Who Has Good News for You

THE WORD

"But how can they call to him for help if they have not believed? And how can they believe if they have not heard the message? And how can they hear if the message is not proclaimed? And how can the message be proclaimed if the messengers are not sent out? As the scripture says, 'How wonderful is the coming of messengers who bring good news!' " (Romans 10:14-15).

THE WORLD

The children and the new pastor or teacher.

Each time we come here for worship, I bring two things for you. One is a message from the Bible; the other is something for you to see. First, I will read you the message from the Bible. As you hear it, see if you can guess what I brought for you to see.

The message from the Bible is "But how can they call to him for help if they have not believed? And how can they believe if they have not heard the message? And how can they hear if the message is not proclaimed? And how can the message be proclaimed if the messengers are not sent out? As the scripture says, 'How wonderful is the coming of messengers who bring good news!' "

From hearing those words, can you guess what I brought for you to see? The words tell us we cannot believe unless we hear a message. We can't hear a message unless someone comes to tell us. When someone does come, it is wonderful if that messenger tells us good news.

This is what I want you to see (*point out the new pastor or teacher; give name and a brief introduction*). _____came here to be a messenger. His [her] message to you is that Jesus is your Savior. The good news he [she] has for you is that Jesus died for your sins and rose again to give you eternal life. He [she] will have lots of other things to tell you but all of them will come from the message that Jesus is your Savior.

Today is a happy day for us because _____ becomes our pastor [teacher]. We agree with our text that quotes the Old Testament prophet Isaiah by saying, "How wonderful is the coming of messengers who bring good news!"

I brought _____ so that you could see him [her] and be happy that he [she] will be with you to bring you good news. But now I also have a message for _____ . I have the same word for you (*name of pastor or teacher*). But I have something different for you to see. Look at these children.

You are here to tell them the good news about Jesus. But the words you heard from Romans also say that you need someone to tell you good news. These children are indeed here to listen to your good news, but they are also here to tell you the good news about Jesus. Part of the joy of your ministry here will be that they will tell and show you that Jesus also loves you.

They are happy about you today; I want you also to be happy about them. When you see them, you can also say, "How wonderful is the coming of messengers who bring good news!"